BITE SIZE ADVICE

ADVICE

SIZE

VOLUME **3**

The Concluding Tutorial ...

Bite Size Advice 3

The Concluding Tutorial … A Final Guide to Political, Economic,
Social and Technological Issues

Paul J. Thomas

GOKO
PUBLISHING

GOKO Management and Publishing
PO Box 7109
McMahons Point 2060
Sydney, Australia
First Edition 2018

Library of Congress Cataloguing-in-Publication Data

Thomas, Paul J.
        Bite Size Advice 3: The Concluding Tutorial ... A Final Guide
        to Political, Economic, Social and Technological Issues

        p. cm.
        IBSN: 978-1-925732-56-6
        LCCN: 2018905734
                BUSINESS & ECONOMICS/General
                BUSINESS & ECONOMICS/Government & Business
                BUSINESS & ECONOMICS/Education

This work is dedicated to my children – Natalie, Justine, Paul, Wesley, Leanne and Jodie – the joys of my life.
You made me poorer, but richer.
Thank you for putting things into perspective.

ALSO BY PAUL J. THOMAS

Bite Size Advice: A Definitive Guide to Political, Economic, Social and Technological Issues

Bite Size Advice 2: The Lesson Continues …
A Further Guide to Political, Economic, Social and Technological Issues

PREFACE

By picking up this book and reading this preface, you have expressed an interest in learning more about the world around us. This compendium is designed to reward that interest by presenting, in one volume, a collection of thought-provoking blog posts covering the key issues impacting our day-to-day lives.

This anthology is also the final volume in a trilogy of books with the generic title *Bite Size Advice.* Like volumes 1 and 2, *Bite Size Advice 3* traverses familiar territory. All three works are punctuated by four common thematic chapters – **P**olitical, **E**conomic, **S**ocial and **T**echnological.

These thematic elements collectively represent a **PEST** analysis – a tool used by businesses to assess threats and opportunities in the environment. For ten years, I have used the PEST framework to categorise the blog posts that I have written as CEO of Gateway Bank (formerly Gateway Credit Union) in Sydney.

At the time of writing, I had published more than 450 online posts. *Bite Size Advice* (1) featured 100 of these posts. *Bite Size Advice 2* showcased a further 100 posts. This book, *Bite Size Advice 3*, gathers an additional 65 posts. The complete set bookends a tumultuous decade that began shortly before the Global Financial Crisis.

If you are a newcomer to the *Bite Size Advice* series, welcome! It's great to have you as part of the family. Please be assured that no prior knowledge of the contents of volumes 1 or 2 is required or presupposed. This tome is not a sequel but a stand-alone text that can be read on its own.

Notwithstanding this, reprinted on the succeeding pages are the Foreword, Introduction and Afterword from volume 1. This was deemed necessary to provide uninitiated readers of the *Bite Size Advice* series with an understanding of the background to the blog and how the posts came to be published in book format in the first place.

To those readers familiar with my work via the first two instalments, welcome back. I am sure that it would be stretching the truth to label you as *Bite Size Advice* devotees. So I will temper my enthusiasm at your loyalty and describe you as informed and inquisitive individuals who want to keep abreast of contemporary issues.

In today's world of time constraints and information overload, staying up-to-date can be challenging, which is why *Bite Size Advice 3* is ideal for the time-starved reader. It delivers informed advice in bite size chunks. This one volume is a business book, an educational book and a general knowledge book.

The blog posts contained in the pages that follow are wide in sweep and bring readers face-to-face with the issues that are shaping politics, impacting economies, transforming societies and driving technology. This multidisciplinary lens provides fresh perspectives on the interplay between a range of PEST issues that are of national and international significance.

Overall, the entire *Bite Size Advice* series can be viewed as a diagnostic tool that shines a light on some of humanity's biggest challenges. In a world which is increasingly interconnected, the subliminal message in many of the posts is that we need to reframe our thinking if we are to create a better planet for future generations.

It is my hope that the broad subject matter will pique your interest and encourage you to read more extensively for yourself. Nelson Mandela, quite rightly, believed that "education is the most powerful weapon which you can use to change the world". The acquisition and sharing of knowledge is indeed a potent force that can help foster peace, eradicate poverty and increase prosperity.

You can be an agent of change by adopting a fresh mindset based on multidisciplinary thinking. Increasingly, the answers to the big global questions cannot be found within single academic disciplines – such as economics – alone. You can play a part in improving public discourse by creating a new type of conversation which moves humankind from *what is* to *what could be* by promulgating an expanded world view.

The posts are deliberately designed to make you think as they tangle and weave through disparate but connected topics. By joining the dots, you will hopefully gain a helicopter view of where individual disciplines intersect and overlap. And by cross-pollinating ideas from a range of fields, you will be able to make new connections and see more creative solutions to contemporary problems.

As for me, I can confidently say that there will not be a fourth instalment of *Bite Size Advice.* This is definitely the end of the line. My days of commenting on the PEST changes taking place in our world are over. This third and final instalment crowns and completes a lifelong yearning to publish and is a fitting conclusion to a decade of researching and writing blog posts.

While my name alone is on the cover of this book, getting it into your hands (or e-reader) was not a solo effort. Every author needs a behind-the-scenes support team and I have had the same four-woman crew for all three volumes of *Bite Size Advice.* Yet again, they have helped me navigate the sometimes-choppy waters of book publishing.

It is a given that every author should acknowledge their publisher and I do so eagerly. Katherine Owen bravely accepted the challenge of turning my blog posts into a book and then a second book and now a third. She is clearly a glutton for punishment and I am glad that we took this journey together. I am indebted to Katherine for taking a chance on me as a writer and for always being so approachable.

While Katherine wrapped a cover around my posts, my unflappable PA, Marisa Dul, firstly swathed them with tender loving care. Marisa is a sharp-eyed proofreader who carefully perused each post looking for errors. She is a most capable and competent assistant and I salute her significant contribution to eliminating mistakes and inconsistencies.

Just as Marisa supports me at work, my wife does the same at home. Beverley has stood beside me throughout my professional career and, more recently, has been the chief cheerleader in my writing endeavours. Beverley happily indulges my desire to write and understands my need to do this on a weekend (due to Monday–Friday work pressures), even though this decreases the amount of free time that I can spend with her. One thing is clear: Without her unfailing support, you would not be reading this now!

Finally, I send an extra special note of gratitude to my Chairman, Catherine Hallinan – and not just because she is my boss. Catherine is a trusted colleague and source of wise counsel. I am honoured to serve as her CEO and wish that there were more leaders with her scrupulous level of honesty and integrity. Catherine is a keen strategic thinker whose unremitting encouragement has been most welcome.

While it is appropriate that I give a shout out to these wonderful women, they are not responsible for the words on the pages ahead. So please allow me at this juncture to append the usual qualification. While every effort has been made to ensure that all the information in this book is correct, I accept full and sole responsibility for any errors which may have crept in.

I should also mention that since the publication of *Bite Size Advice 2*, Gateway Credit Union Ltd has re-branded. It now trades as Gateway Bank Ltd and is part of the new breed of co-operative banks operating in Australia. To be clear, there are two types of banks in the world: those owned by shareholders and those owned by customers. Gateway falls into the latter category.

May I conclude this preface with a brief comment about believing in yourself. The popular literature is replete with simplistic "you can do it" platitudes. Self-help books typically contain step-by-step instructions from self-appointed gurus. The reality is that these "recipe" manuals, which are rarely subjected to scientific scrutiny, promise more than they can deliver.

I know from experience that there are no quick fixes to life's challenges. So, I am not going to offer you gratuitous advice or clichéd motivational quotes about how you can achieve your goals. But what I will say is that with focus and determination, anything is possible, and I am proof of that. As I write these words, I am 60 years of age. It has literally taken me a lifetime to become an author.

Deep down, I was always quietly confident that I would one day publish a book. But other roles – such as being a father – quite rightly took precedence. It was only after our children left home and Beverley and I became empty-nesters that we were both able to pursue personal interests. I am still pinching myself that my dream of becoming an author has now come true three times over.

To be clear, my children did not stop me writing. Rather, I made a deliberate and correct decision to focus on family. The prime responsibility of any parent is to be an effective role model and it's hard to do that if you are absent. Raising my kids and seeing them take their place in society is without doubt my greatest and most important achievement.

I hope that my children are proud of me, because I am full of love for them.

Paul J. Thomas
Sydney, June 2018

This book contains a cross-section of blog posts organised thematically into four chapters. Each chapter contains posts covering a common theme. By arranging the posts into discrete subject areas, the reader can find all the content about a specific topic in one chapter, making browsing by interest much easier. Note that the chapters can be read in any order and that each chapter begins with a brief introduction. Please also note that the posts contained in each chapter are not presented in chronological order. Given this, each post ends with a footnote showing the original publishing date to provide a timestamp and historic context.

CONTENTS

FOREWORD

It is estimated that there are over 150 million blogs on the Internet and the number continues to rise. The blogosphere has rapidly become a big and busy world yet is still relatively new. The first blog was written by a college student in 1994 and a decade later the word blog was declared word of the year by Merriam-Webster.

While there are many blogs, not all are created equal. One which stands out from the crowd is a thought-provoking and eclectic blog written by Paul Thomas. Paul is the Chief Executive Officer of Gateway Credit Union in Sydney[*]. Gateway was a relatively early adopter of blogging and maintains one of Australia's leading business blogs.

---

[*] On 1 March 2018, Gateway Credit Union Ltd became Gateway Bank Ltd.

Australian companies remain cautious about embracing social media tools like blogs. In contrast, Paul has been putting a human face to Gateway via his CEO Blog since March 2008. Paul is living proof that blogging is no longer the sole realm of geeks and believes that corporations without blogs are faceless entities.

This book is a compelling collection of some of Paul's blog posts – 100 to be exact. His weekly posts are a combination of economic commentary, thought leadership and financial hints. What ties these seemingly disparate categories together is that they are all written through the prism of a banking and financial services lens.

Of course, you can't talk about banking without talking about money, since the two are so intertwined. Paul has written about the history of money, the future of money and the creation of money. He has also published posts on money etiquette, money disorders and money management.

Money comes in many forms and Paul has explained the workings of fiat money, credit money and virtual money. He has also outlined how money affects Wall Street and Main Street and how money and debt are two sides of the same coin. He has described the operation of monetary policy and the use of quantitative easing.

As a business blogger, Paul is not an uncritical apologist for free markets because no economic or political system built by humans is perfect. But as an economic rationalist, Paul is proud to nail his colours to the mast and declare that he remains a proud supporter of open markets – even with their imperfections.

To this end, he has published blogs in defence of globalisation, deficits and bailouts. He has stood up for free enterprise and capitalism while underscoring the need for greater ethics and accountability in banking and highlighting the pitfalls of over-regulation.

Along the way, he has pointed out the dangers of excessive leverage, the importance of savings and the need to educate our children and young adults in money matters. From Islamic banking to fractional reserve banking, Paul educates and informs in an easy-to-understand and entertaining way.

The Global Financial Crisis provided Paul with a rich source of developing and unfolding events to comment upon. He explained both the cause of and response to the crisis. The crisis exposed the greedy and destructive side of human nature at both an institutional and individual level.

Paul has a deep understanding of the human condition and is passionate about people and human behaviour. That passion finds expression in the humanistic narrative thread that weaves seamlessly through his blog. Economics is the study of human behaviour as it applies to money and Paul's musings on money and life have touched a chord with a growing readership.

This book's strength lies in its accessibility. Each blog post is succinct and can therefore be digested quickly and easily. This compendium, then, is perfect for the time-starved reader and for those with short attention spans since all posts are concise yet informative.

By avoiding excessive jargon and clearly explaining key concepts, *Bite Size Advice* demystifies key issues which impact our day-to-day lives. It fills a gap in the literature on contemporary political, economic, social and technological issues in a user-friendly way.

You will discover that Paul is a storyteller who eases readers into complex topics while offering authoritative insights and opinions. I am an avid reader of Gateway's CEO Blog which Paul religiously updates every Monday morning to keep it fresh and relevant.

Under Paul's leadership, Gateway has grown from an institution with little brand recognition to a respected name in the financial services sector. He is passionate about Gateway's *"people helping people"* philosophy and believes that credit unions must constantly change while forever staying the same.

Paul has had a long and successful career in financial services. He is a resourceful and strategic CEO who has forged a reputation as a thought leader. An accomplished public speaker and writer, Paul's credentials include an MBA and a Diploma in Financial Services.

In the pages that follow, you will find an informative collection of Paul's blog posts. Persuasive in argument and wide in sweep, they offer a fascinating window into many of the contemporary political, economic, social and technological issues facing society. I hope that you enjoy reading them as much as I did.

C.M. Hallinan
Chairman
Gateway Credit Union Ltd
Sydney, June 2015

INTRODUCTION

Never in my wildest dreams did I think that my blog posts would one day be turned into a book. When I took my first uncertain steps as a rookie blogger in March 2008, I thought that I would quickly run out of steam. Seven years later, I can safely say my concern was unfounded.

I took to blogging like a duck to water and have never missed a weekly posting, even though I still lose sleep worrying about the content of next week's blog! I find blogging extremely rewarding as it enables me to show a more human side to banking and finance.

From the outset, I have used my blog to offer what I hope have been enlightening insights into the often misunderstood world of banking and finance. I have tried to shine an instructive light on the inner workings of a sector that touches the daily lives and wallets of billions of people around the world.

Whether it's taking out a mortgage to buy a home, obtaining capital to start a business, transferring money to electronically pay bills, putting savings away to fund one's retirement or insuring your life and personal possessions, the financial services industry plays a key role.

Indeed, the financial services industry is the hub of an economy, facilitating the productive flow of funds between sectors, companies and individuals. The banking industry plays a critical role in fuelling economic growth by providing credit to households, businesses and governments.

Money, of course, is a central component of our lives and influences practically every decision that we make. We need money to pay for our basic needs (food, clothing and shelter) and to finance our non-essential wants (exotic holidays, luxury cars and designer goods).

Some people are defined by money, others see money as merely a means to an end, while others still have very little money. This economic inequality has driven me to opine on the extremes of wealth and poverty, highlighting the gap between the richest and poorest in society.

Humans love to debate and argue their point. Some high profile debates I have weighed into include the population debate, the climate debate, the welfare debate and the privatisation debate. On a lighter note, I also debated the merits of having a corporate wardrobe.

Maintaining a corporate blog has clearly enabled me to share my ideas and opinions on a range of political, economic, social and technological topics. What I have learned along the way is that you must distil a lot of information into a coherent and cohesive argument or summary.

If the truth be known, I was initially a very reluctant blogger and was dragged into blogging by a colleague who argued that it would be good for Gateway and for me. I find it hard to imagine my professional life without blogging – it's become part and parcel of my working week.

The golden rule of blogging is that you must be authentic, so my blog is an online extension of my personality. My overarching aim is to be an honest and transparent blogger who tries to inform and debate in an entertaining way.

In March 2013, I celebrated my fifth anniversary as a blogger which caused me to look at the blog with fresh eyes. What struck me was that my blog, unlike most others, did not have a name. Choosing a personal blog title was something that I overlooked when my blog was launched.

I was told that the best blog titles are short, compelling and easy to find in search results. So, I chose to name my blog *Doubting Thomas*. The term "doubting Thomas" can be viewed in a negative or positive light depending on whether you are a destructive cynic or a constructive sceptic, and I am the latter.

Cynicism is a mindset of automatic doubt, whereas scepticism employs critical thinking to determine validity. The word sceptic is from the Greek word *skeptikos* which means to inquire or find out. It is said that scepticism (factual analysis) is the best way of seeking the truth.

The French mathematician, scientist and philosopher René Descartes (1596–1650) insisted on thinking for himself rather than simply accepting what he had been taught. He resolved to hold nothing true until he could be absolutely certain of it.

Descartes eventually discovered that the one thing he could never doubt was the fact that he himself existed, since the very act of doubting required a doubter. He expressed this conclusion in the now famous Latin phrase *"Cogito, ergo sum"* – "I think, therefore I am." To paraphrase Descartes, "I think, therefore I blog."

Finally, please note that each blog post was originally written to be read independently of the rest. Given this fact, some repetition and overlap occurs when stand-alone posts covering the same topic – albeit from different angles – are reproduced together in this one book.

POLITICAL
INFLUENCES
1

Like it or not, you can't escape politics. Every day, around the world, governments make decisions that affect our day-to-day lives. Politicians determine how much tax we pay, what laws we obey and how much money the state spends on essential services like roads, education and healthcare. The blog posts in this opening chapter focus on the radical policy agenda of Donald Trump and his unorthodox political positions on trade, immigration and foreign policy. The president's divisive leadership style, his use of social media and his impact on the political landscape are also examined.

HATEpolitics

Brexit and the US election will be remembered as the two big political events of 2016. Both demonstrated how the world – in a political sense – has lurched to the far-right. In an increasing number of countries, the radical right – a group of extremist parties united by their hatred of immigrants – has been surging in popularity.

Many voters have moved towards the far-right as part of a nationalistic wave that has swept the US and Europe. This shift has been led by Donald Trump in the US, Nigel Farage in Britain, Marine Le Pen in France and Geert Wilders in the Netherlands. (Of course, we have Pauline Hanson in Australia.)

These populist parties and their followers have been variously described as racist, xenophobic, anti-Islamic and anti-refugee. Their divisive and toxic ideology has propelled them from flash in the pan protest parties to serious players on the political field that have taken centre stage in elections.

Parties of the far-right focus on tradition – real or imagined – and play on a nostalgia which yearns for simpler times. They want to turn back the clock to when national cultures were not influenced by immigration (and globalisation) and jobs were the preserve of native-born citizens.

This delusional hankering for the good old days was epitomised in Donald Trump's right-wing rallying cry to "make America great again". Apparently, this greatness will be achieved by closing borders, curtailing trade and building a wall to keep out Mexicans.

We should not forget that it was this kind of old-fashioned nationalism that helped fuel two world wars. However, since 1950, the burgeoning growth in international trade has helped make the world a more peaceful place. Yet, far-right-wingers favour economic nationalism (protectionism) over global free markets.

Free trade is built on voluntary interactions of buying and selling, and this encourages nations to live in harmony. Free trade raises the cost of war by making nations more economically interdependent. The more people rely on trade with others, the greater the cost to all parties of a conflict.

The rise of the far-right coincided with the onset of the Global Financial Crisis (GFC) in 2008. During prosperous times, workers tolerate the free movement of capital and labour. However, they arc-up in the face of mass job losses, falling living standards and harsh austerity measures.

The GFC inflicted these conditions on society, bringing despair to millions. The far-right has fed off their enduring economic misery. Angry voters have abandoned mainstream political parties as they are seen to be unsympathetic to the plight of workers.

Rising income and wealth inequality have pitted Wall Street against Main Street. The divide between the haves and have-nots has widened, creating a class of people suffering acute economic anxiety. Poverty and hardship have become the lot of an increasing number of Americans and Europeans.

When people are scared about their future, they look for someone to blame. They are angry at what they see as government inaction to solve their economic problems. They are in crisis and feel that they have been deserted by the very people elected to help them.

Given this mindset, the right-wing backlash is not surprising. Indeed, history teaches us that economic hard times fuel political extremism, as it did in the 1930s following the Great Depression. Populist movements have been most successful during weak economic times. According to a 2015 study:

> Over a period of nearly 150 years, we have seen that every financial crisis was followed by a 10-year surge in support for far right populist parties, as shown by a recent analysis of more than 800 elections by German economists.

The rise of the new radical right reflects a deep social and economic malaise affecting an increasing number of nations. The past decades have ushered in an unprecedented level of socio-economic change, and voters are expressing their dissatisfaction at the ballot box.

Only time will tell how long this anger and resentment lasts. What is clear is that the rhetoric of the far-right has struck a chord with a critical mass of voters. They have transformed the political landscape and become a force to be reckoned with.

Hang on tight, as our journey to the far-right continues for the foreseeable future. Indeed, we do live in interesting times.

POSTING DATE | 21 NOVEMBER 2016

4

TRADEwars

A US think-tank predicts that Donald Trump's protectionist policies will spark a trade war, push America into recession and destroy 4.8 million American jobs by 2019. The Peterson Institute, based in Washington, D.C., is one of many voices sounding a warning bell about Trump's intention to impose prohibitive tariffs on international trade.

A cross-section of political and economic wonks – including commentators, academics and journalists – has expressed concern about the impact of Trumponomics on the global economy. Many fear that the centrepiece of Trump's macro-economic agenda, "America first", will backfire and hurt the very people it is designed to protect – the working class.

While the cost of living for all Americans would rise because of a trade war, the have-nots would suffer more than the haves. This is because the less you earn, the more tariffs hurt as you are forced to spend a greater proportion of your income on more expensive goods. How the little guy would fair under tariffs was outlined in a *Wall Street Journal* article:

> Nobody wins in a trade war. If Donald Trump sparks one with China, among the losers will be some of his most ardent supporters: blue-collar workers who helped sweep him to election victory. In fact, they'll stand to lose twice. They've already endured stagnant incomes for decades amid withering trade competition from China.

Trump's threatened tariffs of 45 per cent on all Chinese imports would hit their pocketbooks again by raising the price of pretty much everything on sale in Wal-Mart, from sneakers to microwave ovens. Nor is there convincing evidence that punitive tariffs would bring back jobs lost to China. The march of technology has altered the employment landscape. American factory workers are threatened more by automation than Chinese sweatshops.

Workers in the American heartland voted for Trump as they felt left behind by the forces of globalisation. In reality, robots and automation have cost more blue-collar jobs than trade. Notwithstanding this inconvenient truth, the president-elect is focussing on trade as the culprit and this will have adverse consequences for America and the global economy.

Some of these consequences were identified in an opinion piece prepared during the US election campaign by another Washington, D.C.-based think-tank, Third Way. In *50 Ways Trump Is Wrong on Trade,* Third Way captured the sentiments of "50 leading experts, publications, and outlets that have come out in opposition to Trump's views on trade".

Their collective voices warn of a stock market collapse, a new recession on par with the Great Recession, massive job losses, rampant inflation and a ballooning trade deficit. All agree that protectionism is dangerous and debunk and rebuke Trump on trade. Here are two quotes from the Third Way article.

USA Today Editorial: Trade produces more affordable merchandise and more variety, a godsend for consumers struggling to make ends meet. It is also responsible for significant amounts of employment: 11.7 million people in America work in export-related industries. And protectionist measures, such as the huge tariffs that Trump tosses around, would ignite trade wars that would do far more economic harm than good.

Brookings Institution, Financial Times: A Trump administration would pose the greatest shock to international peace and stability since the 1930s. He also opposes every trade deal America has signed over the past 30 years. He wants to use tariffs and other protectionist measures to bludgeon other countries into accepting lopsided agreements that disproportionately benefit the US. Under his presidency, the open global economy would slam shut.

During the election campaign, edition after edition of *The Economist* magazine was justifiably critical of Trump. The 7 May 2016 print edition stated that Trump "subscribes to a set of protectionist and economically illiterate policies that are by turns fantastical and self-harming".

Ripping up old trade agreements and imposing massive new tariffs will likely set off a trade war that will have the precise opposite effect of liberalised trade – prices will rise and growth will slow. We can only hope that Trump's pronouncements on trade are no more than a sabre-rattling negotiating tool and that his protectionist policies are not implemented.

As a check-and-balance against Trump's extremism, it is important to note that the Republican Party is not historically anti-trade and that the party retains control over both the US Senate and House of Representatives. So, there's good reason to hope that we will avoid economic Trumpageddon.

POSTING DATE │ 5 DECEMBER 2016

COURTINGtrouble

Let's be frank: Donald J. Trump is a divisive figure. The billionaire property developer won the race for the White House against all odds. He has no experience in government and is the first non-politician to be elected president since Dwight Eisenhower.

In defiance of nearly every opinion poll, Trump pulled off a stunning upset. The ill-disciplined reality TV star flouted virtually every convention to defeat Hillary Clinton in a polarising campaign. His behaviour made him the most talked-about political figure of 2016 and *Time* magazine's Person of the Year.

To many, it is unfathomable that his campaign did not self-destruct after his lewd and vulgar remarks about women were made public. Despite his sexist insults and other jaw-dropping statements, Trump prevailed. His slurs, innuendos and hyperbole did not sink his presidential candidacy.

Many of the things he promised in order to get elected make no sense. His flimsy policies appealed to the heart, not the head. A disgruntled electorate voted on emotion, not logic. The working class were conned by Trump, who tapped into the social undercurrents that exist in the "divided states" of America.

In his efforts to secure his spot as the 45th president of the United States, Trump declared war on his own party, called for a ban on Muslims entering America, labelled Mexicans "rapists" and "drug dealers" and vowed to slap a 45 per cent tariff on Chinese imports.

If that were not enough, he threatened to throw Hillary Clinton in jail, declared that women who seek abortions should be punished, claimed he knew "more about ISIS than the generals" and boasted that he would be "the greatest jobs president that God ever created".

Controversial filmmaker Michael Moore claimed that Donald Trump never actually wanted to be president. US Vice President Joe Biden also theorised that Trump did not want to win the presidency. Trump himself said in a 1987 *Time* interview: "I have no intention of ever running for president".

Whether he wanted it or not, Trump will soon be the leader of the free world. At 70, he will be the oldest person in history to be sworn in as US president. Those who argued that "Trump for President" was a ruse that was going to last only for a short while are still scratching their heads.

The next four years will be a very interesting social experiment. Trump will enter the White House riding a wave of xenophobia and will take the reins of a divided nation. Over recent decades, Americans have never been more bitterly split – particularly over immigration and globalisation.

Can we expect to see more of the provocateur Trump we witnessed on the campaign trail? Or will the new president be more statesman-like? My sense is that over the next four years the world will be subject to the whims of one very unpredictable man and this will give rise to many concerns.

Personally, I hope that Trump does not start a trade war with China. I hope that he does not declare climate change a hoax. I hope that he does not build a great wall. I hope that he does not suppress freedom of the press. Most of all, I hope that he does not start a nuclear war.

Like millions of others, I worry that the US will have an angry finger on the nuclear button. This finger will belong to a temperamental commander-in-chief who pledged during the election campaign to "bomb the shit" out of ISIS and to significantly increase US military spending.

My suspicion is that buyer's remorse will eventually grip the US public. Trump will continue to rewrite the rules of politics and his unorthodox ways will unsettle many. His followers will eventually come to realise that most of Trump's campaign promises were implausible.

POSTING DATE │ 12 DECEMBER 2016

PLANETtrump

Donald J. Trump is now the leader of the free world. He was sworn in as the 45th president of the United States of America on 20 January. A new world order has begun. Game changing disruption is upon us. Everything is up for grabs. The world is set to be reshaped.

It's not possible, however, to say precisely what the new president will actually do. He flip-flops on virtually every issue and has turned self-contradiction into an art form. He changes his tune with regular monotony and thinks absolutely nothing of walking away from a previously-stated position.

His about-faces and back-downs are breathtaking. You could be forgiven for thinking that no one disagrees more with Donald Trump than Donald Trump himself. Here are some of the president's contradictory utterances:

"I have no intention of running for president." (*Time*, 14 September, 1987)

"I am officially running for president." (New York, 16 June, 2015)

"I don't want it for myself. I don't need it for myself." (ABC News, 20 November, 2015)

"I wanted to do this for myself. … I had to do it for myself." (*Time*, 18 August, 2015)

"If I ever ran for office, I'd do better as a Democrat than as a Republican – and that's not because I'd be more liberal, because I'm conservative." (*Playboy*, March 1990)

"I'm a registered Republican. I'm a pretty conservative guy. I'm somewhat liberal on social issues, especially healthcare." (CNN, 8 October, 1999)

Research by NBC News reveals that during his bid for the White House, Donald Trump took 141 distinct stances on 23 major issues. With regard to abortion, he pivoted between five different positions in three days. He also has a muddled position on gun control with a foot in each camp.

Trump constantly shifts position because he is a showman who plays to the crowd. He whips the audience into a frenzy by telling them what they want to hear. For the former reality TV star, the presidential campaign was a stage where he bantered back and forth with his fans.

In reality, many of his proposals are either unrealistic in terms of executive power or may be blocked by Congress. Trump has many enemies in the Senate, even among his own Republican party, and they are unlikely to rubber stamp his policies out of party loyalty. However, some policy changes – like climate change and immigration – can be done to varying degrees by the Trump White House on its own.

A key Trump campaign pledge was to undo Barack Obama's ambitious climate change policies. The new president does not accept the environmental evidence that climate change is real and wants to abandon the Paris climate change accord. In 2002, Trump tweeted that "the concept of global warming was created by and for the Chinese in order to make US manufacturing non-competitive".

Regarding immigration, Trump will need funding from Congress if he is to build his big border wall to keep out the Mexicans. In contrast, his crackdown on illegal immigration will take only a stroke of the presidential pen. Through executive action, he has undertaken to deport up to three million undocumented immigrants, but this requires resourcing. Trump's promise to triple the number of Immigration Enforcement and Customs Agents will be expensive and so needs congressional authorisation and appropriations.

In his 100-day plan published in October, Trump vowed to reverse – in one fell swoop on his first day in the Oval Office – every one of Obama's executive actions. On the campaign trail Trump said: "The good thing about an executive order – I walk in, sign, I don't have to go through Congress". Presidential life, as Trump will learn, is not so simple. It will take some time for the new president to tear down the Obama legacy.

However, one thing from the Obama administration that Trump did ditch on his first day in office is the Trans-Pacific Partnership trade deal. In November, Trump stated: "I am going to issue a notification of intent to withdraw from the Trans-Pacific Partnership – a potential disaster for our country". Shortly after President Trump was sworn in, his administration announced the US withdrawal from the 12-nation TPP trade pact.

At this early stage of Trump's presidency, the only thing that is certain is the uncertainty he will create. He will upset the status quo and put his own unorthodox stamp on the office of president. His lack of political experience means that he will continue to manage by the seat of his pants, putting America and the rest of the world into unchartered waters.

He will undoubtedly be a controversial president. He entered the Oval Office with the lowest approval rating of any president-elect in four decades. My fear is that we will have a front row seat to a slow-moving train wreck. Along the way, we may well see the US lose its claim to be a credible world leader. I truly hope that I am wrong and that President Trump modifies his tone and behaviour.

POSTING DATE | 30 JANUARY 2017

FOREIGNpolicy

Donald Trump's election has shaken the world's geopolitical order. His approach to international affairs is upending the foreign policy playbook. Many of his pronouncements are at odds with the principles underpinning the liberal global order in place for more than 70 years.

With no experience in foreign affairs, President Trump is tossing aside the normal protocols of international relationships. He caused uproar in Beijing when he accepted a phone call from the president of Taiwan and he stunned many when he voiced admiration for Russia's Vladimir Putin.

Ignoring allies and praising enemies is not the way diplomacy is supposed to be done. Yet this modus operandi is not out of step for a president with a reputation for breaking with tradition. He uses Twitter to make policy announcements and press conferences to jawbone critics.

America's new diplomat-in-chief has an enigmatic approach to world affairs. It is difficult to discern a coherent worldview as his policy positions have not been detailed in extensive white papers. *The Washington Post* labelled Donald Trump's foreign policy inexperience as "a true liability".

We know that President Trump wants to redefine his nation's role in the world to "make America great again". But nationalist platitudes about greatness and saving domestic jobs do not add up to a strategic doctrine. Mr Trump's foreign policy utterances offer no clear overarching philosophy.

A recent edition of *The Economist* magazine accused President Trump of underestimating the fragility of the global economic system and of misreading geopolitics. It stated:

> He has casually disparaged the value of the European Union, which his predecessors always nurtured as a source of stability. He has compared Angela Merkel, Germany's chancellor and the closest of allies, unfavourably to Vladimir Putin, Russia's president and an old foe. He has savaged Mexico, whose prosperity and goodwill matter greatly to America's southern states. And, most recklessly, he has begun to pull apart America's carefully stitched dealings with the rising superpower, China – imperilling the most important bilateral relationship of all.

The Economist goes on to warn that "alliances that take decades to build can be weakened in months". President Trump acts as though countries are like businesses and that diplomacy between states follows the art of the deal. But he is unlikely to get what he wants from sovereign nations by picking fights.

Among other things, Mr Trump has called NATO "obsolete", imposed a travel ban on seven Muslim-majority countries, encouraged the breakup of the European Union, undermined free trade agreements, challenged the one-China policy and promised to bolster America's nuclear capability.

If that were not enough, he has also threatened to "bomb the shit out of ISIS", pledged to move the US embassy to disputed Jerusalem, committed to deploy more US military forces to the South China Sea, vowed to "rip up" the nuclear deal with Iran and blasted his own intelligence agencies.

With such a fragmented policy agenda, many believe that President Trump is creating a "New World Disorder". While the president wants "America First", he might well get "America Alone" if he persists in isolating the US from her long-standing allies.

"If rejecting traditional allies was not dramatic enough," opines US think-tank, The Brookings Institution, "Trump also sees Russia as a logical partner" in fighting Islamic State. Mr Trump brushes off concerns about Russia's aggressiveness in Ukraine and Europe and rejects claims that the Kremlin interfered with the US election.

Washington, D.C.-based publication *The Hill Extra* believes that Mr Trump's election "represents what could be the biggest geopolitical shakeup in the global order since the collapse of the Soviet Union 25 years ago". At a minimum, his election heralds the start of an era of global uncertainty and volatility.

America's new commander-in-chief has not been tested in a crisis and many worry that his impulsive nature might drive him to hit the nuclear button. To mitigate this risk, a new bill banning the president from first use of nuclear weapons without a Congressional Declaration of War has been submitted to congress.

During the election campaign, Mr Trump tweeted that it was time for the US to start stockpiling nukes again. He also asked, "why can't we use nuclear weapons?" after stating a wish to "nuke" Islamic State militants. Further, he urged Japan and South Korea to build nukes, reversing decades of US policy.

The president sees himself as a strongman and the concern is that he may use the tools of his high office to enforce his will. Certainly, his war overtures have unsettled many. But does this really mean that we are moving closer to nuclear apocalypse? According to atomic scientists, the answer is "yes".

The group behind the famed Doomsday Clock recently moved it forward by 30 seconds. It now stands at 2½ minutes to midnight. This is the closest the clock has been to Doomsday since the 1953 when both the US and the Soviet Union, as part of the Cold War, tested thermonuclear bombs.

Nuclear poker is a dangerous game and a sure-fire recipe for making the world a less safe place. Here's hoping that cool heads prevail and that no one rolls the thermonuclear dice.

POSTING DATE │ 6 FEBRUARY 2017

UNPRESENTIALtwittering

Barack Obama was the first presidential candidate to understand the power of social media. He used it to garner support and get people engaged. Donald Trump went further in harnessing the power of social media. He used it as an online soapbox to reach millions of voters.

Social media is an undisputed fact of modern life and exerts significant impact on society. Public debate is now dominated by social media and it influences the national discourse. You need look no further than the recent US presidential election to see what a game-changer it is.

Donald Trump used social media to outgun his opponents with his weapon of choice – Twitter. During the presidential campaign, tweeting gave Mr Trump uninhibited access to voters and enabled him to portray himself as the people's champion. This positioning was integral to his success at the polls.

Every time Mr Trump tweeted something outrageous, the reaction was immediate. Many of his tweets went viral, appearing on the home page of major news outlets. Experts estimate that this helped generate $2 billion worth of free media for "The Donald", providing a significant boost to his profile.

Mr Trump not only used Twitter to promote himself but also to take down opponents. His aggressive use of Twitter to attack his presidential rivals was unprecedented. He taunted, mocked, vilified and denounced anyone – even from his own party – who stood between himself and the Oval Office.

Myriad critics have slammed Mr Trump's use of Twitter. He has the dubious honour of being a master at the art of trolling. He left many breathless at the amount of vitriol he was able to squeeze into each 140-character broadside. Protesters around the world found his online trash-talk unacceptable.

Barry Burden, a political science professor at the University of Wisconsin in Madison, observed that Trump's "aggressive and unconventional use of the (Twitter) platform generated news" even when his tweets "violated standard norms of campaigns by being uncivil, conspiratorial or offensive".

In an article titled 'The role of technology in the presidential election', *The Economist* magazine explained how social media helped Mr Trump win the presidency:

> He (Trump) and Steve Bannon, his controversial campaign boss and now his chief strategist, understood how the Facebook and Twitter-driven media landscape worked. Whether a piece of news spreads online does not depend on whether it is true and coherent, but whether it is surprising, shocking and confirms prejudices. It can bounce endlessly in virtual echo-chambers - even if it is patently false.

An opinion piece in *CIO Magazine* explains that social media acts as glue for like-minded people and reinforces confirmation biases. Moreover, it brings out the darker side of digital introverts and often amplifies slanted views and political biases while showcasing voter/follower ignorance.

Fabricated stories that favoured Donald Trump were shared on social media a total of 30 million times. This, according to Stanford economist Matthew Gentzkow, is nearly quadruple the number of pro-Hillary Clinton shares leading up to the US presidential election.

Social media was replete with misinformation about the campaign. Fake news stories gave life to utterly false claims like "Pope Francis shocks world, endorses Donald Trump for president" and "FBI agent suspected in Hillary email leaks found dead in apartment in murder-suicide".

Politicians have always manipulated the facts. But what we saw in the US election was something new and frightening – completely made-up stories. Bald-faced lies (e.g. Hillary Clinton is running a child sex ring out of a pizza shop) were disseminated online to large audiences willing to believe the fictions and spread the word.

Most disturbingly, fake news – according to political fact-checking website *PolitiFact* – "found a willing enabler in Mr Trump who at times uttered outrageous falsehoods and legitimized made-up reports". Dishonesty in politics is nothing new, but Mr Trump has taken it to a frightening new level.

PolitiFact rated more of his statements "pants-on-fire" lies than any other candidate. So, did voters really believe Mr Trump when he claimed that President Barack Obama "is the founder" of Islamic State? Did they not challenge his assertion that Ted Cruz's father might have been involved with Lee Harvey Oswald?

Mr Trump's litany of blatant lies and smears put him in a league of his own. One US newspaper recently asked: "If the president and his aides will tell easily disproven falsehoods about crowd sizes at his inauguration, what other 'alternate facts' will they be willing to disseminate?"

Truth, logic and consistency no longer seem to count for very much when it comes to politics. Mr Trump is held to a different set of rules than other politicians. He has been allowed to get away with behaviour that would have doomed all other presidential campaigns.

Trump's words are designed to do one thing: fire up voters. During the campaign, his rhetoric convinced a critical mass of Americans to vote for him. His supporters wanted change and he promised to deliver it. The rest of us are still trying to get over the political shock of a click-and-elect president.

POSTING DATE | 13 FEBRUARY 2017

POLITICALdivide

2016 was a year of electoral surprises. Britain voted to leave the EU, the US sent Donald Trump to the White House and the Italians rejected a referendum on constitutional reform. In each case, anti-establishment parties hailed the results, claiming that they marked the beginning of a new world order.

Between now and September, elections will be held in the Netherlands, France and Germany. Further victory for populism will add momentum to the steady march of far-right nationalism – a movement that has swept up swaths of the world's population. We are witnessing the collapse of the liberal world order, a system based on open borders and open societies.

The liberal world order was created in the aftermath of World War II. Liberalism is an international (as distinct from national) worldview that opposes isolation and protectionism. The liberal vision looks for collective solutions to global problems by working co-operatively with the help of international institutions and alliances to make the world a better place.

Whereas liberalism as a political ideology is linked to globalisation, nationalism is driven by anti-globalist sentiments. Nationalists want a more homogenous society and tighter controls by governments over territory and borders. The mantra of nationalist politicians – "country first" – fuels calls to build fences and erect trade barriers.

One of the hallmarks of liberal internationalism is rule-based relations which are enshrined in institutions, such as the United Nations. However, under nationalism, we would see a more contested and fragmented system of economic blocs and regional rivalries. The desire to increase sovereign control invariably results in isolationist policies, particularly with regard to immigration.

In his final address to the UN General Assembly on 20 September 2016, Barack Obama delivered a stinging rebuke to those who would build walls saying: "A nation ringed by walls would only imprison itself". In the same speech, he defended liberal globalisation arguing that open markets, capitalism and democracy should remain the guiding forces of the international order.

> I believe that at this moment we all face a choice. We can choose to press forward with a better model of cooperation and integration. Or we can retreat into a world sharply divided, and ultimately in conflict, along age-old lines of nation and tribe and race and religion. I want to suggest to you today that we must go forward, and not backward. I believe that as imperfect as they are, the principles of open markets and accountable governance, of democracy and human rights and international law that we have forged remain the firmest foundation for human progress in this century.

It is paradoxical that the growing calls for a less open world would actually hurt the poor most of all. Since the end of World War II, free trade has lifted millions out of extreme poverty. It is irrefutable that globalisation has been good for the global poor. This point was also made by President Obama.

The integration of our global economy has made life better for billions of men, women and children. Over the last 25 years, the number of people living in extreme poverty has been cut from nearly 40 per cent of humanity to under 10 per cent. That's unprecedented. And it's not an abstraction. It means children have enough to eat; mothers don't die in childbirth.

President Obama went on to say that "our international order has been so successful that we take it as a given that great powers no longer fight world wars; that the end of the Cold War lifted the shadow of nuclear Armageddon; that the battlefields of Europe have been replaced by peaceful union".

This worldview is not shared by President Trump who has declared that "Americanism, not globalism, will be our credo". Ironically, Donald Trump's plan to take "retaliatory economic action" against China will backfire. His China trade plan will result in American families paying a lot more for food, clothing, electronics and everything else labelled "Made in China".

Populist politicians are undermining liberal internationalism, and this poses a threat to peace and prosperity. Less international co-operation will lead to increased distrust between nation-states and may even give rise to conflict. Nativism and its beggar-thy-neighbour policies is a backward and dangerous step for the world.

In the words of the adage, it really is a case of "united we stand, divided we fall".

POSTING DATE | 27 FEBRUARY 2017

OPINIONpolls

Following last year's Brexit referendum and the US election, the spotlight fell on polling companies. On both sides of the Atlantic, the pundits failed to predict voter rejection of the status quo. The electorates of Britain and America threw up unexpected results that called into question the reliability of pollsters.

Despite expert forecasts to the contrary, the UK voted to self-eject from the European Union and underdog Donald Trump claimed the White House. In the space of less than five months, upsets at the ballot box – reflecting a sea-change in global politics driven by populist movements – were not picked up by political analysts.

Many believe that the polls led us down the garden path, with Britain voting for the unfathomable and Trump performing better than expected. Consequently, David Cameron, the architect of the "remain" campaign, resigned and presidential candidate Hillary Clinton did not get to occupy the Oval Office.

Polls consistently underestimated the level of support for Brexit and "The Donald", with both ultimately emerging victorious. Myriad columnists, think-tanks and political strategists have undertaken post-mortems to explain why the polling data was wrong. Each has their own theory as to why predictions missed their mark.

Regarding the US election and its "unplanned presidency", one hypothesis is that the polls did not accurately capture the true voting intentions of an army of hidden Trump supporters. These individuals were apparently too embarrassed to admit – even anonymously – that they planned to back the controversial celebrity businessman.

Educational backgrounds also played a major part in the US election as they did in the UK referendum. During a traditional election, pollsters gauge voter sentiment based on left or right leanings. However, the way people voted in the referendum turned on educational lines. The less educated overwhelmingly backed Brexit. Conversely, areas where more residents had higher education skewed sharply to remain in the EU.

Education has become a fundamental divide in democracy. There is clear evidence of a correlation between one's level of education and political affiliation, causing a split between graduates and non-graduates. Both British and American election pollsters underestimated the ideological divisions along a growing fissure – the education fault-line.

There are, of course, other factors at play in the recent spate of surprise voting results around the world. Technology is one and demography is the other. Advances in telecommunications and changes in demographics have made it more difficult for pollsters to get an accurate read on voters' intentions.

In today's high-tech world, we communicate differently. Mobile phones have usurped traditional landlines while social media competes with conventional news outlets. Younger adults, in particular, have embraced new ways of consuming and sharing information. They use mobile apps and Internet sites like Facebook as their prime news sources.

It is argued that social media – not traditional phone polling – holds the key to being able to understand the voice of the people. Classic polling cannot accurately capture anger or enthusiasm. Therefore, most pollsters did not detect the large swathe of the electorate in both Britain and America who felt disenfranchised and left out. One of the few companies that accurately called the US election did so by analysing social media posts and the underlying sentiments behind them (e.g. the angry Midwest in the US).

For decades, polling organisations were able to accurately tap into public opinion simply by calling people at home. Landline phone numbers were generated at random and nearly every home had a phone. As more than 70 per cent of those contacted were willing to participate, it was easy for pollsters to find a representative sample of likely voters.

Nowadays, large segments of the population have given up their landlines for mobile phones. Landlines are quickly going the way of the telegraph with fewer and fewer homes having a fixed line. This is making it increasingly difficult for pollsters to reach people who get all their calls on mobile phones and are reluctant to answer calls from unfamiliar numbers.

People who have landline phones are demographically different from people who don't, and demographics play a huge role in deciding elections. Regarding Brexit and the US election, we saw the usual demographic divides such as *age* (young versus old), *geography* (city versus country) and, in the US, *race* (non-white versus white).

But insufficient attention was paid to the millennial demographic and other online groups who "live" on social media.

The recent US election was the most polled event in history. Yet the views captured were not representative of the electorate at large. This does not mean that polls are headed for the graveyard, but that polling methods must change. Traditional polls have been discredited while social media has come of age. Pollsters need to get on the social media bandwagon if they are to obtain more representative and trustworthy feedback from the electorate.

POSTING DATE │ 6 MARCH 2017

IMMIGRATIONpolitics

Few contemporary issues are more controversial than immigration. It emerged as a top issue in the 2016 US presidential election campaign. It was a driving force behind Brexit and the desire to restrict entry into the UK. And it has propelled right-wing parties in France and elsewhere that campaign on a "no more immigrants" platform.

Anti-immigration sentiment is alive and well in many nations. Around the world, hard nationalist and xenophobic politicians have galvanised support by whipping up fear over immigration. This fear is breeding hostility and creating divisions between communities. Asylum seekers and ethnic minorities have become targets of intolerance.

Debate about immigration has moved from the margin to the mainstream over recent years. A growing number of nations are putting up the "house full" sign to curb the movement of people between countries. The rising backlash against immigration shows no signs of abating – it is a global phenomenon that has changed the political landscape.

This change was partly fuelled by the Global Financial Crisis (GFC) which created deep wounds that have not healed. Renowned economist Nouriel Roubini argues that the "weak recovery (post-GFC) has provided an opening for populist and protectionist parties to blame foreign trade and foreign workers for the prolonged malaise".

Consequently, we are now suffering a backlash against globalisation and the freer movement of goods and labour.

Many economists believe that immigrants are being used as scapegoats. Migration, no matter how controversial politically, makes sense economically. Immigrants contribute more in taxes than they receive in benefits, according to the OECD.

A new IMF study shows that migration drives up economic growth and boosts productivity in advanced economies. Both high and low-skilled workers who migrate bring benefits to their new home countries by increasing income per person and living standards. The report found that a 1 per cent increase in the migrant population creates an extra 2 per cent GDP per capita in the long term.

A Migration Council of Australia report underscores that the economic impact of migration flows through into every aspect of our economy. The report states that "for too long the economic contribution of migration to Australia has been significantly undervalued". The report goes on to say that "by 2050, migration will be contributing $1,625 billion to Australia's GDP".

A prominent Australian economist believes that migrants may be our greatest economic asset. Migrants lift the three Ps of economic growth: population, participation and productivity. Population refers to the number of people of working age, participation identifies how many of those people actually work, while productivity measures each worker's level of output.

Those who challenge the merits of immigration are often unaware that most advanced economies are heavily reliant on immigrants for labour growth. That's one of the reasons why Angela Merkel welcomed so many working-age refugees into her country. Germany has an aging labour force and a declining birth rate and desperately needed an injection of young workers.

For years, German industry has been complaining that it cannot find enough young people to fill vacant positions. This need is also evident in many other nations. Yet one of the most well entrenched myths about migrants is that they steal jobs from native-born workers. The faulty logic that is used to prosecute this myth is called the "lump of labour fallacy".

This fallacy is premised on the erroneous assumption that the amount of work available in an economy is fixed and that no one can get a job without taking one from someone else. It's an understandable assumption, but it's wrong. Immigrants who gain work also gain income to spend, creating new jobs. Immigration, therefore, increases the demand for labour and stimulates employment.

Commenting on the positive impact that immigrant workers have on the US economy, *The New York Times Magazine* explained that imported workers:

> use the wages they earn to rent apartments, eat food, get haircuts, buy cellphones. That means there are more jobs building apartments, selling food, giving haircuts and dispatching the trucks that move those phones. Immigrants increase the size of the overall population, which means they increase the size of the economy. Logically, if immigrants were "stealing" jobs, so would every young person leaving school and entering the job market; countries should

become poorer as they get larger. In reality, of course, the opposite happens.

So the conventional wisdom which says that immigrants take jobs and lower wages is absolutely wrong. In reality, immigrants create jobs and make native workers more prosperous. As world-renowned economist and Nobel laureate Paul Krugman commented, "the (lump of labour) fallacy makes a comeback whenever the economy is sluggish".

The world is clearly better off when goods and services and people cross borders. Yet it seems that statistics alone won't win the current immigration debate. Regrettably, arguments based on emotion are trumping those based on reason. When logic flies out the window, good judgment and the ability to make informed decisions goes with it.

POSTING DATE │ 27 MARCH 2017

CHINArising

It's a massive worldwide project. It spans more than 65 countries. It will cost over $US1 trillion. And it will redefine global trade. It's being led by the Chinese and is the brainchild of China's president, Xi Jinping. It's quietly reshaping the world, but you probably haven't heard about it.

In 2013, China announced what is arguably the most ambitious political and economic initiative ever undertaken by a single country. President Xi revealed plans to commence a vast program of infrastructure building throughout China's neighbouring regions to create two new foreign trade routes. The stated aim is to connect major Eurasian economies through infrastructure and trade.

Known as the One Belt, One Road (OBOR) initiative, it's reminiscent of the ancient Silk Road trading routes. The 21st century version is a combination of land-based and sea-based trade connectors. The "belt" is a network of overland road and rail routes (the Silk Road Economic Belt). The "road" is a network of ports and other coastal infrastructure projects (the Maritime Silk Road).

OBOR will see China build a web of infrastructure – railways, roads, ports, pipelines, bridges, energy systems and telecommunication networks – that will more thoroughly connect China with the economies of Europe, Asia and the Middle East as well as emerging markets in Africa. OBOR will also cement China's influence among Pacific nations like East Timor, Fiji and Papua New Guinea.

If China's massive transcontinental infrastructure drive succeeds, it will rewire global trade and create the world's largest economic platform. Moreover, it will usher in a new world economic order. To quote *The New York Times:*

> It (OBOR) is global commerce on China's terms. Mr. Xi is aiming to use China's wealth and industrial know-how to create a new kind of globalization that will dispense with the rules of the aging Western-dominated institutions. The goal is to refashion the global economic order, drawing countries and companies more tightly into China's orbit.

> The projects inherently serve China's economic interests. With growth slowing at home, China is producing more steel, cement and machinery than the country needs. So Mr. Xi is looking to the rest of the world, particularly developing countries, to keep its economic engine going.

Some commentators have compared the OBOR initiative to the Marshall Plan. This plan saw America provide vast amounts of aid to regenerate European Allies after World War II and to insulate the Soviet Union. OBOR is said to be 12 times bigger in absolute dollar terms than the Marshall Plan.

In contrast to the Marshall Plan, OBOR is based on 21st century economic development, not 20th century Cold War alliances. China is spending hundreds of billions of dollars in the hope of winning new friends around the world, without requiring military obligations.

China's OBOR initiative has been a widely discussed topic in geopolitics since it was proposed by President Xi. It's a subject of hot debate and has both opponents and supporters. Critics see it as a massive expansion of Chinese imperial power that will fuel the rise of a new Chinese empire. Enthusiasts contend that it will boost the economies of less developed regions and lift millions out of poverty.

Reality, as is typically the case, lies somewhere in between. My sense is that China is using her financial clout to help poorer nations become wealthier so that they can buy Chinese products – an apparent win-win. But nations do not want China's funding at any cost. In November, Pakistan and Nepal both pulled out of deals to build dams with China because of disagreements over the terms of the deals.

Over the past three decades, China has undergone an astounding transformation. It has gone from an inward-looking nation mired in poverty to an emerging superpower that rivals the US. China achieved this status by becoming an industrial powerhouse via low-cost manufacturing producing toys, apparel, electronic goods and textiles for the world. Now it is morphing again, this time from the world's factory to the world's builder.

China is expected to pass the US economically in the next decade. As well as soon boasting the world's biggest economy, China may also be able to claim that it has encircled the world thanks to the OBOR. Significant-ly, China's rise to global pre-eminence will be a peaceful one, without bloodshed.

Some argue that China's growth strategy is based on the philosophy of the ancient Chinese strategist Sun Tzu. His 1,500-year-old text, *The Art of War*, is a paradox. Despite its name, the book teaches how to avoid conflict and win battles without fighting. This makes modern China a harbinger of world peace.

At the recent world economic forum in Davos, the contrast between America's nationalist agenda and China's global outlook was stark. Mr Trump's remarks focussed on encouraging inbound investment in the US while Chinese leaders proposed a new global economic system.

It's hard to fathom how America's global retreat will trump China's great outward leap. It is President Xi, not President Trump, who is making his nation great. The global economic order is shifting, and history will judge Mr Trump harshly for closing off America's economy from the world.

There will undoubtedly be many twists and turns along China's belt and road. The journey will be challenging but the rewards great. My suspicion is that we will need to modify our language from "all roads lead to Rome" to "all roads lead to Beijing".

POSTING DATE | 26 MARCH 2018

UNELECTEDpower

You probably haven't noticed because it's so subtle. But it's real and it's gathering pace. Over recent years there has been a faint but powerful transfer of public power from elected politicians to unelected officials. This delegation of authority to unelected technical experts and independent authorities is occurring around the globe.

The world is moving towards a more distributed power structure where non-government organisations (NGOs) are gaining influence at the expense of nation-states. NGOs have moved from backstage to centre stage in world politics. Their influence in international relations and policymaking is largely uncontested and is transforming politics.

The war on terrorism, the fallout from the Global Financial Crisis (GFC) and action on climate change have all contributed to an increase in the power of unelected officials. Our planet may be divided into 193 sovereign nations, but we live in a world that is deeply interconnected and interdependent. The threats we face are common and require a co-ordinated, collective response.

Given this, we are increasingly turning to experts outside of government and inside of NGOs to guide and shape state decision-making. Consequently, there has been a proliferation of international standards over recent years which most governments have simply incorporated in their national laws. In the words of one academic:

Every-day life of businesses and consumers is pervaded by the references to global private standards: from the cars we drive to the computers we use, from the food we eat to the movies we watch. Private rule-making at the transnational level is increasingly gaining scope and traction, quickly expanding in both old and new territories, from e-commerce to data protection, from food safety to human rights protection, from financial markets to environment, from professional regulation to corruption and anti-money laundering, from civil aviation to private security.

NGOs are a worldwide phenomenon and can push around even the largest governments. Some label this power shift to unelected technocrats as "illegitimate authority" and a danger to domestic sovereignty. Others see the growing prominence of specialised unelected bodies as an integral and positive part of modern democratic life.

Globalisation has spawned the growth in organisations that regulate and control activity on a global scale. An example is the activities of the International Accounting Standards Board. It sets transnational financial reporting rules that corporations around the world follow, making it a powerful (but private) de facto global regulator of accounting standards.

Many believe that an even more powerful body is the Basel Committee on Banking Supervision. This Committee, which is headquartered at the Bank for International Settlements in Basel, Switzerland, makes decisions which affect every man, woman and child on the planet. Yet few know of the existence of this unelected and (some would add) unaccountable group of central bankers and banking supervisors.

The Basel Committee does not possess any formal supranational authority and its decisions do not have legal force. Yet its views hold great sway, enabling it to impose stringent rules and standards on the global financial system. *The Economist* magazine described central bankers as "more powerful than politicians, holding the destiny of the global economy in their hands".

Beyond banking and accounting, NGOs address every conceivable issue and operate in virtually every part of the globe. From buying bananas at the supermarket (the World Trade Organisation governs how bananas are traded) to obtaining medicine at the chemist (the World Health Organisation issues standards for prescription drugs), international laws impact our daily lives.

Imagine flying overseas to watch a major sporting event. The operation of the plane that transports you is regulated by the International Civil Aviation Authority. On arriving at your destination, you drive to your hotel by following standardised road signs developed by the UN Convention on Road Traffic. Following check-in, you phone home and this global connectivity is facilitated by a treaty on International Telecommunication Regulations.

You leave your hotel and use your credit card to buy a jacket and this transaction is governed by technical requirements issued by the Payment Card Industry Security Standards Council. With your jacket to keep you warm, you then watch an outdoor event (as part of the Olympic Games) where athletes are subject to mandatory drug testing by the World Anti-Doping Agency.

NGOs are a worldwide phenomenon and there is no turning back the clock. I accept that these non-state actors (to use the language of academics) are essential to the smooth working of our globalised world. However, I also add my voice to those who believe that NGOs should be more transparent in their decision-making and subject to greater checks and balances. The underlying question here is: Who regulates the regulators?

The reality is that those who write the rules in international private organisations encounter little push back. This is acknowledged by Tim Büthe & Walter Mattli, authors of *The New Global Rulers: The Privatization of Regulation in the World Economy*. They note:

> An ever-increasing share of economic activity is governed by international rather than domestic rules or standards, often developed by private bodies. Frequently, such global private regulation entails no market competition among multiple rule-makers. Instead, a single organization serves as the clear institutional focal point in its area of expertise and is largely uncontested in making the rules for global markets. As a result, once such a private-sector body develops a standard, it becomes the global rule.

While I understand the motivation to have one set of common rules for global markets, I nonetheless express concern at the one-size-fits-all approach as has occurred with banking regulation. The Basel Accords were primarily intended for internationally active and systemically important banks. But the same regulatory standards have been applied to smaller financial institutions like credit unions.

The efforts by regulators to bolster financial system stability and avoid a repeat of the GFC turmoil are laudable. Few would challenge the goal of a more resilient banking sector. But care must be taken not to punish those, like credit unions, that did not engage in the reckless behaviour that contributed to the GFC.

POSTING DATE │ 4 SEPTEMBER 2017

PARLIAMENTARYsystems

Successive Australian governments have not been able to govern effectively. They have been hampered from enacting their policies by an obstructionist upper house. Minor parties and independents have captured enough Senate seats to thwart, delay and cause chaos in our federal parliament.

Like many voters, I believe that when a government wins office it should be able to implement its election commitments. However, under our two-tier system of government, that is wishful thinking. A ruling party's mandate – won at the polls – does not stop the upper house from blocking legislation.

Australia has a bicameral legislative system. In a bicameral system of government, authority is shared between two separate chambers. In many legislatures worldwide, these chambers are colloquially described as the lower house and the upper house.

More formally, they bear different names in different jurisdictions. Examples of lower house titles include House of Representatives, House of Commons, Chamber of Deputies and Federal Assembly. In contrast, upper houses are sometimes called the Senate, House of Lords or Federal Council.

Not all countries have bicameral legislatures – a number have adopted unicameralism. A unicameral parliament is a legislature that consists of one chamber or house. Supporters of the unicameral system believe that two chambers are redundant and obstructive and that one is more efficient.

Approximately half of the world's sovereign states are unicameral, including our close neighbour New Zealand. The Kiwis adopted a unicameral system in 1951 and it serves them well. Post the Global Financial Crisis (GFC), the New Zealand economy has outperformed every other OECD economy.

NZ Prime Minister John Key has been able to implement serious structural reforms, including welfare changes, part-privatisations and tax mix switches. These economic reforms have ushered in a new wave of Kiwi prosperity and resulted in plucky New Zealand punching above its weight.

Many commentators argue – quite rightly – that Key has been able to swiftly implement his promised policies as he has no upper house impeding his reforms. In stark contrast, Australian prime ministers need to deal with a Senate that has become increasingly recalcitrant.

In this tale of two nations, Australia is being left behind as serious political and economic reform has ground to a halt due to a hostile Senate. Minor parties continue to hold the balance of power in our upper house and act as power brokers for any policy that is presented.

The result of this crossbench kingmaker behaviour can be seen in many policy areas including taxation. While tax reform has been central to New Zealand's rebirth, Australia has put it in the "too-hard" basket. Yet our current tax structure is fiscally unsustainable and needs to be overhauled.

Last year, the Canberra-based think-tank The Australia Institute issued an instructive paper titled 'Who really makes legislation?' Among other things, the paper noted the following:

- Food is exempt from the GST because the Democrats refused to support a GST at all unless their amendments were agreed to by the Howard government.

- In exchange for voting for the privatisation of Telstra, Mal Colston quit the ALP to be promoted to the deputy presidency of the Senate by John Howard.

- Independent Senator Brian Harradine was famous for holding up national legislation unless he got some lollies for Tasmania.

- During the GFC, Nick Xenophon delayed the passage of the $42 billion stimulus package until he got an extra $900 million for the Murray River.

Frankly, there is something fundamentally wrong with a political system that enables a minority of upper house politicians to hold a popularly elected government to ransom. No wonder former Prime Minister Paul Keating famously described the Senate as "unrepresentative swill".

Dissatisfaction with the Senate is not new. In a 2008 article titled 'Why Australia needs a less powerful Senate', La Trobe University lecturer Ian Tulloch had this to say:

> What Australia needs is a less powerful Senate, a Senate which cannot block supply and cannot unduly hold up the legislation of the government of the day. Long ago the British House of Lords

lost its power to defeat legislation. Australia should follow suit. The only legitimate function of the Senate is the review of legislation. It was originally supposed to be a 'states rights' house, however the domination of the party system has effectively rendered this role redundant. The review role could just as easily be done in the House of Representatives with an expanded committee system. After all New Zealand has managed quite well with just one house.

Australia is in desperate need of parliamentary reform, but don't hold your breath waiting for change. The chances of us getting a single-chamber Australian federal parliament any time soon are zero. Legislative success will continue to depend on the government's ability to herd cats.

It remains my faint hope that one day we will admit that the current system has passed its use-by date and do something about it. Meantime, we will see more forced deal-making and the serving of vested interests. Such behaviour is an embarrassing blight on our parliament democracy.

POSTING DATE | 26 SEPTEMBER 2016

POLITICALlife

Being a politician is a tough and thankless job. The hours are long, the pay is unremarkable and the environment is demoralising. You must put up with a cynical electorate, a distrusting press and a hostile opposition. You are always on-call and everything you do and say is dissected.

Few of us could stand the heat of being under such constant scrutiny in both our public and private lives. Yet that is the plight of our elected officials. Always in the spotlight and forever the target of critics, our politicians quickly learn to develop a thick skin.

Around the world, it has become a national sport to hate politicians. They are near the top of the most detested professionals in the eyes of the public. As a matter of routine, our much-maligned politicians are abused, scorned and ridiculed and are often seen as indecisive and untrustworthy.

I am not an apologist for politicians who are inept or corrupt. However, I believe that we have unrealistic expectations of what they are able to deliver. Politicians are not miracle workers who have the power to solve all of society's ills.

Yet some in the electorate have the erroneous expectation that it is the government's responsibility to give them a job, raise their children, keep them slim and look after them in their old age. Former Treasurer Joe Hockey referred to this attitude as "the age of entitlement".

The number and complexity of the problems our political leaders face daily would cause most of us to buckle under the strain. As elected representatives of their communities, our politicians know that they can't please everyone and that's why politics is the art of compromise.

As the great Roman orator and politician Cicero remarked: "How easy it is for those who play no part in public affairs to sneer at the compromises required of those who do". Politicians also know that the public often doesn't want to hear the truth.

For example, the Australian household sector is currently the most indebted in the entire world. No politician, of course, would be game to criticise families for that level of debt, nor suggest that they are living beyond their means. Households, on the other hand, openly berate the government for Australia's level of sovereign debt which, paradoxically, is one of the lowest in the world.

It's clear that there are double standards at play here and this is challenging for our leaders. Australian leadership experts Geoff Aigner and Liz Skelton weigh into this debate in their book, *The Australian Leadership Paradox: What It Takes To Lead In The Lucky Country*. The authors note that:

> Australians bemoan the quality of our leaders. We blame those in power for not showing leadership, only to turn on them when they start tackling the hard issues they are expected to fix. No wonder that even the most passionate and talented among us hesitate to take up this important role.

Nowadays, opinion polls and minority groups unduly influence policy formulation resulting in long-term economic credibility being sacrificed for short-term populist reforms. The result is that the public gets policies that are against their own best interests.

We all have a say in voting governments in and politicians should be worthy of the people they serve. Equally, we have an obligation to behave responsibly and avoid short-term community hysteria just because we don't get our way on a particular issue.

Right now, we need to make some very hard decisions in Australia. For example, we need to reform our taxation system as it is fiscally unsustainable. But how many Aussies would vote for a leader who wanted to raise taxes? I would, because I know how imperative it is, but I suspect that I would be in the minority.

An informed electorate is a prerequisite for democracy to be effective. Yet many people are uninformed about the workings of government. On the other side of the coin, we need to attract competent people to hold positions of political power. Demand for top talent is subject to the law of supply and demand, so top performers don't come cheap.

The US president – considered the most powerful person in the world – earns less than many people who hold mid-ranking corporate jobs. The same holds true in Australia. I believe that we need to pay our politicians more to attract the best and brightest. But how many voters would agree with that?

With populist politics sweeping the world, one could be forgiven for thinking that citizens don't want bold and inspirational leaders who are prepared to make hard decisions for the greater good. That's why it's largely our fault if we end up with poor political leadership.

As French political philosopher Alexis de Tocqueville observed: "In democracy, we get the government we deserve".

POSTING DATE │ 10 OCTOBER 2016

NANNYstate

It only ever happened on one occasion, but I still vividly remember it. I was 13 years of age and a student at a Catholic college. I received one stroke of the cane and so did every other boy in the class. But, like 95 per cent of my classmates, I had done absolutely nothing wrong.

The teacher was upset that a couple of boys were misbehaving. Whenever the teacher turned his back to write on the blackboard, two students were disruptive. As the teacher could not identify the culprits, he chose to punish the entire class.

The teacher's decision all those years ago to discipline every boy is an example of collective punishment. Today, most academic experts agree that it is unfair to hold all students accountable for the misdeeds of a few troublemakers, but this is exactly what happens in contemporary society.

Punishing many citizens – via rules and regulations which limit our freedoms – for the misdemeanours of the minority has become the norm. This lowest-common-denominator thinking has resulted in blanket laws that assume the worse behaviour of everyone.

I am not a drinker* but am subjected to random breath testing (RBT) as a driver. I am not a terrorist but must undergo mandatory bag screening and metal detection scanning as a traveller. I am not a pervert but am prohibited

---

* For the record, I am a teetotaller. Also, for the record, I accept that travellers are subject to security checks at airports, but object to the way passengers are treated by officious security personnel.

as a grandfather from taking photos of my family at the municipal swimming pool.

Research confirms that RBT does have a deterrent effect as a law enforcement practice, but it has not stopped drink driving. In contrast, increased airport security checks are viewed as "theatre" by prominent aviation experts and as "redundant" by the chairman of a major airline. When it comes to stopping parents and grandparents taking photos of treasured moments, authorities are seen as overzealous.

All nanny state interventions take the guise of protecting us from harm. It's a form of paternalism which treats citizens like subordinates. But to what extent should the whole community be forced to adhere to laws that are really aimed at controlling the behaviour of a small segment of the populace?

One answer to this question can be found in the writings of English moral philosopher John Stuart Mill. He believed that a competent person's freely-made decision should never be overridden, even for that person's own good. In his seminal text *On Liberty*, Mill wrote:

> ... the only purpose for which power can be rightfully exercised over any member of a civilized community, against his will, is to prevent harm to others. His own good, either physical or moral, is not a sufficient warrant. He cannot rightfully be compelled to do or forbear because it will be better for him to do so, because it will make him happier, because in the opinion of others, to do so would be wise, or even right.

Put simply, Mill believed that individuals should be free to make their own choices even if those choices are considered by others to be reckless or bad. This position accords with the view of independent Australian senator and libertarian David Leyonhjelm, who launched a parliamentary inquiry into "the nanny state". According to Leyonhjelm, "harming yourself is your business, but it's not the government's business".

Personally, I accept that governments have the right to interfere in our lives when our behaviour – like domestic violence – harms others. But if a cyclist chooses not to wear a helmet while riding a push bike or a pedestrian chooses to jaywalk when crossing the road – and these risks are confined to the individual concerned – why should they be fined and treated as a criminal?

As an ocean swimmer, I sometimes wonder whether one day the government will pass a law requiring me to wear a life vest in the surf. If that ever happens, it would undoubtedly result in fewer ocean swimmers, just as there are now fewer bicycle riders following the introduction of the mandatory requirement for cyclists to wear a helmet.

After two decades and copious research, there is still no compelling evidence that Australia's compulsory helmet laws have reduced injury rates on a population-wide basis. Commenting on this issue, a recent UK health magazine article stated:

> After Sydney introduced a helmet law in 1991, the number of cyclists on the roads plummeted because many erstwhile cyclists couldn't or wouldn't buy a helmet. Research has shown

that cycling becomes more dangerous when there are fewer bikes on the road and motorists tend to leave cyclists less room when they are wearing a helmet. The result? Fewer people got to enjoy the health benefits of cycling and there was a higher rate of accidents among those who remained.

Australia has three levels of government, all of which like to meddle in our lives. It's not surprising that we have been accused of becoming the world's most over-regulated country. Increasingly, we can't have fun at our own risk and it seems that everyone is being held accountable for the actions of others. Also, enforcing unnecessary rules on law-abiding citizens means that real crime gets a free pass.

Life is about choices. I fear that the rising tide of rules and regulations will eventually strangle life.

POSTING DATE │ 9 MAY 2016

ECONOMIC TRENDS | 2

Economics is a social science. It's the study of human nature as it applies to money. It focusses on the behaviour and interactions of households, businesses and governments and their attitudes to saving, investing and spending. The monetary choices made by these economic agents impact markets and this is reflected in the topics covered in this chapter. In addition to examining share markets, housing markets, currency markets and market bubbles, this chapter also contains posts that deal with broader macroeconomic issues including government deficits, sovereign ratings, deflation risks and austerity measures.

DEFENDINGcapitalism

It has been called the greatest engine of material prosperity in human history. It has lifted people out of poverty. It has raised living standards. It has funded research to cure diseases. It has given us better nutrition. It has driven mind-blowing innovations. It has revolutionised the way we live and work. And it has provided us with access to goods from around the world.

Capitalism has done all these things and more, which is why I believe it is a force for good. Capitalism has made the world a better place by alleviating human suffering. Today, we enjoy lives that are longer, healthier and better. This is largely because of advances in science, medicine, agriculture, technology and industry. These advances have been driven by the foundation stone of a capitalist economy – private enterprise.

Central to a capitalist system is international trade and this, according to the capitalist peace theory, offers a path to world peace. Free trade is built on voluntary interactions of buying and selling and this encourages nations to live in harmony. Free trade raises the cost of war by making nations more economically interdependent. The more people rely on trade with others, the greater the cost to all parties of a conflict.

The essence of capitalism is economic freedom. Individuals and businesses are free, within the bounds of the law, to engage in commerce at their will and peril. The father of modern economics, Adam Smith, asserted that economic behaviour is driven by self-interest. The Global Financial Crisis (GFC) painfully revealed that the pursuit of self-interest does not always lead to outcomes that benefit society overall.

So yes, capitalism is not perfect, but that's because human behaviour is not perfect. Economic theory is premised on the assumption that humans make rational choices. However, the GFC showed that we don't always weigh facts objectively when making financial decisions. Regarding the ill-conceived subprime lending programs, borrowers, bankers and brokers were united in the delusional belief that house prices never go south.

Another criticism of capitalism is that it leads to inequalities of wealth and income. Again, this is absolutely true and it's an undeniable fact that the rich are getting richer. But the poor are not poor because the rich are rich. The two conditions are generally unrelated. The rich did not steal their wealth from the poor. While some do inherit their fortune, most people work very hard to make their money – it has little to do with luck.

Taxing the rich more is not the solution to inequality. Around the world, higher income workers already pay the overwhelming majority of taxes. In the words of Abraham Lincoln, "You can't make the poor rich by making the rich poorer". To paraphrase Warren Buffett, we all live far better lives because of Henry Ford, Steve Jobs, Bill Gates and the founders of Google. These brave individuals helped expand the economy and this assists the poor as much as the rich.

An open-market, capitalist economy does not deliver equal economic status for everyone. People receive varying financial rewards for the jobs they do and the contribution they make to society. While excessive greed benefits no one, trying to make all of us financially equal is a recipe for disaster. Capitalism rewards productive achievement and provides the necessary incentive for entrepreneurs to take risks and innovate, and this benefits society overall.

Even if we somehow managed to redistribute wealth so that every adult in Australia had exactly the same amount of money, it would be fleeting. The smart, the strong and the devious would quickly acquire the wealth of the slow, the weak and the gullible. Also, people would use their money in different ways. The prudent would save and invest their money while the irresponsible would likely squander it.

The world has seen several socio-economic systems including slavery, feudalism, socialism, communism and capitalism. For all its imperfections, most believe that capitalism, like democracy, is better than the alternatives. Thanks to capitalism, humanity is doing better than it ever has. While we still have problems to solve, they are less severe than at any time in history.

As for those nations suffering severe poverty, they must be helped and encouraged to adopt capitalism. The uneven distribution of wealth in the world is due to the uneven distribution of capitalism. Swedish writer Johan Norberg makes this very point in his book, *In Defense of Global Capitalism,* wherein he states:

> The poor countries that have liberalized their economies have shown impressive results, while those that have not are stuck in deep misery. Therefore, we need more capitalism and globalisation if we want a better world, not less.

Capitalism offers a practical way to nourish the hungry. Handouts are not the solution to poverty in places like Africa. As Bill Clinton noted: "No country can work itself out of poverty with aid alone". Training and assistance must be provided to Africa's private sector to help them drive economic growth and make Africa self-sufficient. Capitalism can do this and more.

POSTING DATE │ 11 JULY 2016

DEFICITmyth

Politicians constantly draw false parallels between household budgets and government budgets. Our elected leaders love trotting out the familiar line that governments – like households – need to live within their means. Yet every time they espouse this untrue analogy, they display their ignorance of economics.

Around the world, ill-informed politicians claim that governments should somehow have a balanced budget year-to-year. Politicians show empathy with the electorate by promising to cut government spending in line with belt tightening by households. Governments that run deficits are accused of being poor financial managers.

Balancing the national budget sounds appealing and promising to get it back in the black resonates with many voters. However, policymakers should avoid playing populist politics by trying to imitate family budgets. Fiscal austerity is commendable at a household level but can equate to economic irresponsibility at a sovereign level.

As counter-intuitive as it sounds, governments do not always need to have a balanced budget. In fact, they can run prudent annual deficits indefinitely, as many countries do. Britain has maintained a national debt for more than 300 years. Going back to 1776, the US has been in continuous debt except for seven short periods.

Government deficits are not intrinsically bad. Indeed, they can be very helpful to an economy. Spending more when the private sector is flagging is a necessary function of government. Deficit spending – through tax cuts or the purchase of goods and services by the government – can help turn an economy around.

Nobel prize-winning economist Joseph Stiglitz argues that deficit spending can be a major stimulus to economic growth and can actually lower long-term government debt. When economic growth is restored and unemployment falls, tax revenues increase which eventually lessens the need for a government to borrow.

Another world-renowned economist and Nobel laureate, Paul Krugman, has often observed that government finances are not like personal finances. While consumers on a spending spree ultimately have to pay the piper, a government's borrowing strategy directly affects economic growth and this delivers social benefits.

A US professor of politics adds to the richness of this debate by noting that government spending has a "crowding in" effect that actually encourages more private investment:

> That is because much of the money that the government borrows and spends goes to the private sector. Private industry must then prepare to provide the various goods and services demanded by the government … In order to do this, these businesses must invest in new production facilities and greater productivity. This "crowding in" effect thus helps to mitigate any negative effects that public borrowing has on the private sector by indirectly encouraging more private investment and business growth.

[NB: To be clear, there are two measures of sovereign debt: *current budget deficit* and *national public debt*. When a government spends more than it collects in any one year, a budget deficit exists. The accumulation of deficits over many years creates the national public debt.]

It can be seen that the debt and deficit narrative is an emotive political construct which does not reflect any underlying economic truth. In the cold light of day, most people would admit that it is more important to create jobs than to reduce the deficit. Balancing the budget does not of itself guarantee growth.

The economy can be likened to a car. Government spending is the accelerator and taxes are the brakes. It follows, therefore, that to speed up the economy you hit the accelerator and to slow it down you apply the brakes. While driving too fast can lead to hyper-inflation, countries invariably slowdown in time.

Let's say that the Australian government needs to spend $50 billion more than it is bringing in from existing tax programs. It could, of course, increase personal and business taxes to cover this shortfall. But raising taxes is politically unpopular, plus it leaves taxpayers with less disposable income.

It follows that if we have less to spend on goods and services, businesses will suffer. If sales fall sufficiently, firms might even reduce their workforce. Those without jobs will, in turn, have reduced spending power and so a vicious cycle begins. So, a preferred way for the government to raise the money it needs is to issue bonds.

Bonds can be thought of as another form of money and governments are the sole monopoly issuer of their money. Households cannot issue money, only governments can. This means that government debt is not like private debt as it never needs to be paid off. As bonds become due, they are replaced with new bonds.

As noted by one economics professor, households – unlike governments – can't roll over debt indefinitely. Also, governments cannot be subject to foreclosure or repossession while households can. Moreover, households can go bankrupt while sovereign governments only default when they choose to do so.

It should be noted that government debt is an incredibly safe investment. Governments, therefore, can borrow money at really low interest rates. In fact, many can borrow at rates lower than inflation. This means that their debt decreases over time in terms of its real value, rather than increasing like household debt.

I'll leave the final word on this emotive topic to University of Melbourne research economist Warwick Smith. In a 2014 article titled 'Why the federal budget is not like a household budget', Smith unequivocally stated that it is a myth to believe that Australia must have a balanced federal budget. He went on to say that:

> Like many myths, it does have some factual historical origins. Back when currencies were backed by gold it was possible for governments to go broke. Because modern currencies are not backed by anything material, sovereign

governments cannot run out of money and can never be insolvent in their own currency. Somehow, mainstream political thinking hasn't kept up with the dramatic changes in the monetary system that occurred more than 40 years ago.

Hear, hear.

POSTING DATE │ 19 SEPTEMBER 2016

AUSTERITY delusion

Economists love intellectual debates. They often disagree with one another and fail to reach consensus on important issues. Following the Global Financial Crisis (GFC), they have been duelling over how to fix the global economy. On one side are economists who believe that government spending is the problem, while on the other are those who believe it is the solution.

This bitter dispute over the role of fiscal policy has seen an old chestnut resurface – is it better to cut spending and raise taxes in an economic downturn or spend your way out of it? Those in the spend-less camp are advocates of *fiscal austerity* while those who favour spending more are proponents of *fiscal stimulus*.

At the heart of this debate are two macroeconomic schools of thought: Keynesian economics and free-market economics. Both sides offer seemingly strong and sound claims to prove that their position – to spend or not to spend – is right. These well-articulated ideological divisions make it difficult for us mere mortals to know which side, if any, has the slam-dunk argument.

Keynesian economists derive their name from the great British economist John Maynard Keynes. They believe that flagging economies require a fiscal boost in the form of more government spending. Keynes himself asserted that aggregate demand – the sum of spending by households, businesses and the government – is the most important driving force in an economy.

In contrast, free-market economists (aka Monetarists) advocate a government "hands off" policy, rejecting the theory that government intervention in the economy is beneficial. They prefer to let the marketplace itself sort out any economic problems that may occur and believe that monetary policy alone is capable of taming business cycles.

The passage of time post-GFC has shown that the Monetarists have expected too much of monetary policy. Central banks have run out of ammunition to spur growth in the economy. Despite releasing a range of new weapons – low/zero interest rates and quantitative easing – central bankers have not been able to discourage saving and encourage borrowing.

The good news is that more can be done to jolt economies from their low-growth, low-inflation stupor. In the words of *The Economist* magazine:

> Plenty of policies are left, and all can pack a punch. The bad news is that central banks will need help from governments. Until now, central bankers have had to do the heavy lifting because politicians have been shamefully reluctant to share the burden. At least some of them have failed to grasp the need to have fiscal and monetary policy operating in concert. Indeed, many governments actively worked against monetary stimulus by embracing austerity.

In an earlier article titled 'Stimulus v austerity', *The Economist* explained how fiscal stimulus delivers a multiplier effect which assists an ailing economy:

A dollar spent building a railway, for example, might go to the wages of a construction worker. He then spends the extra income on groceries, enriching a shopkeeper, who in turn goes shopping himself and so on. Every dollar of stimulus could thus result in two dollars of output - a multiplier of two … That allows governments to deliver a hefty economic bang at moderate fiscal cost.

World-renowned economist and Nobel laureate Paul Krugman has consistently argued that more fiscal stimulus is necessary in most economies right now. Despite being criticised by other economists, the prevailing consensus is that Professor Krugman has been proven right. Governments around the world have discovered that slashing spending in the face of high unemployment was a mistake.

In a paper that Professor Krugman authored last year, *The Austerity Delusion*, he states that "it's foolish and destructive to worry about deficits when borrowing is very cheap and the funds you borrow would otherwise go to waste". In Australia, as in other nations, infrastructure spending is a great way for governments to boost the economy.

Infrastructure is the backbone of future economic growth and right now in Australia we have a $500 billion backlog in infrastructure investment which can be reduced with an expansionary fiscal policy. With Australian government bond yields at record lows, there has never been a better time for the federal government to be borrowing more to help reduce this backlog.

However, we Aussies have an irrational and emotive attitude to government debt, even though we have one of the world's lowest debt-to-GDP ratios. Another Nobel laureate and leading global economist, Joseph Stiglitz, had this to say about our attitude to public debt.

> Instead of focusing mindlessly on (budget) cuts, Australia should instead seize the opportunity afforded by low global interest rates to make prudent public investments in education, infrastructure and technology that will deliver a high rate of return, stimulate private investment and allow businesses to flourish.

The idea of not spending more than you have is seductive but dangerous when it comes to public finances. Equally, saying that you can't cure sovereign debt with more debt is powerful but not true. Interestingly, the populist policies of the major political parties in the recent Australian elections saw both pledge to reduce debt – exactly the opposite of what we need!

POSTING DATE │ 18 JULY 2016

MARKETbubbles

As children, we were taught that what goes up must come down. As adults, we often ignore this sage advice when it comes to investing and money matters. Like the good times, a rising market can't last forever. All trends end, making price corrections (declines) inevitable.

While no one likes to lose money, corrections are commonplace. They are part of the investment landscape and allow a market to pull back on overpriced valuations. Savvy investors welcome a dip in the market and use it as a hunting ground to seek out assets at prices that are not inflated.

By taking the heat out of a market, corrections help ensure that asset prices do not get out of sync with their intrinsic value. Price slumps also help ward off speculative bubbles. History shows that when the price of an asset skyrockets to unsustainable levels, a harsh correction (crash) may be on the way.

Spectacular gains have a habit of turning into devastating bubbles whenever investor enthusiasm for an asset class reaches fever pitch. Irrational exuberance among investors propels a surge in the price to a lofty height which is unwarranted by the fundamentals of the asset.

A common element that runs through most bubbles is the lapse of judgment by individuals whose illogical behaviour becomes contagious. Other investors blindly follow the crowd as the market races higher and are led astray in making the same poor investment choice.

This herd mentality (madness of the crowd) helps explain why speculative surges in asset prices develop. Rising prices attract the attention of a wider audience who see others getting rich – and they want a piece of the action! As explained by Investopedia, an asset bubble – like a snowball – feeds on itself.

> When an asset price begins rising at a rate appreciably higher than the broader market, opportunistic investors and speculators jump in and bid the price up even more. This leads to further speculation and further price increases not supported by market fundamentals. The real trouble starts when the asset bubble picks up so much speed that everyday people, many of whom have little-to-no investing experience, take notice and decide they can profit from rising prices. The resulting flood of investment dollars into the asset pushes the price up to even more inflated and unsustainable levels.

Investor mob psychology is evident in all bubbles and each provides a cautionary tale about getting caught up in financial hysteria. When one person's flawed judgment influences another person's investment decision, errors compound and a bubble forms.

The first recorded capitalist speculative bubble occurred in the 1630s in Holland. Known as the Dutch tulip bulb mania, it saw working-class folk buy flower bulbs for extraordinary sums of money until, without warning, the market for them dramatically collapsed.

Frenzied buying reportedly resulted in one particular bulb selling for as much as a mansion in a fashionable Amsterdam neighbourhood. The rare and exquisite bulbs had become status symbols and people clamoured to get their hands on one. Prices reached the point of lunacy and the bubble ultimately burst.

Less than a century after the tulip craze, overzealous investors watched their life savings vanish when the South Sea Company collapsed in 1720. Yet again, people flocked to an irrationally exuberant market after speculation mania about "Britain's hottest stock" swept throughout the nation.

The South Sea Company was granted a monopoly on trade in the South Seas in exchange for assuming England's war debt. The company's executives exaggerated the commercial value of its trading rights causing its shares to soar, thereby fanning enormous interest in the stock.

One notable investor swayed by the hype was Sir Isaac Newton. The scientific genius who invented calculus and formulated the laws of gravity lost most of his fortune on a stock that briefly defied gravity. He reportedly stated: "I can calculate the motions of stars, but not the madness of men".

Between Newton's loss and now, there have been numerous market crashes. Most readers will recall the dotcom bubble that formed in the late 1990s. Investors became overly optimistic about technology companies and inflated their values. Excitement over the new Internet economy clearly got out of hand.

And who can forget the financial calamity that was the Global Financial Crisis. A US housing collapse triggered the worst economic crisis since the Great Depression. Herd mentality was again at work with home buyers influenced by the purchasing behaviour of others. Americans outbid their neighbours in a desperate rush to get onto the fast-rising housing ladder.

When it comes to investing, history shows that humans are hardwired to stampede with the crowd and the latest example of this is Bitcoin mania. The cryptocurrency's meteoric rise displays all the signs of a textbook bubble – naïve investors with misplaced confidence placing huge bets on something they truly don't understand because everyone else is taking a punt on a new digital asset.

In mid-December, the value of a single Bitcoin rocketed to a staggering US$20,000 driven by self-reinforcing price gains. This was nosebleed territory and a giant throw of the dice for gullible investors who had been lining up to pour money into the latest craze. (Bitcoin dramatically dropped below US$13,000 in the immediate run-up to Christmas.) Most Bitcoin buyers are millennials and they clearly have a different risk appetite to baby boomers.

Many commentators and central bankers are understand-ably raising a red flag, believing that Bitcoin will end in tears for many. It is now the biggest bubble in history and only time will reveal how long this wild ride will last. When the crest is reached and the bubble pops, the downward roller coaster ride will leave a trail of misery.

As Newton discovered, markets can't defy gravity forever. Yet each generation believes that "this time will be different" and that upward trends never end. It's clear that when it comes to investing, humans are predictably irrational, thereby making periodic bouts of chaos inevitable. Which just proves the adage that those who fail to learn from history are doomed to repeat it!

POSTING DATE │ 12 FEBRUARY 2018

SOVEREIGNrating

The potential loss of Australia's coveted AAA credit rating has the scaremongers working overtime. Being downgraded one notch – from AAA to AA+ – is apparently a national disgrace. We are being told to brace ourselves for a dire political and economic crisis.

Well, I for one don't understand the gloom and doom merchants. They are exaggerating the importance of a stamp of approval from a credit ratings agency. A downgrade may be a hit to our national pride, but the likely effects will not be catastrophic.

Claims of a doomsday scenario are at odds with the view of most economists who see a triple-A rating as a second order issue. According to *The Australian*, the cost of Australia losing its top-notch AAA credit rating would be far greater for politicians than for the economy.

Policymakers view the threat of a downgrade to Australia's sovereign rating as a shot across the bow. It represents a warning to the government and is seen as a political blow. If a downgrade does occur, it would be used by the opposition as "proof" that the government cannot manage the economy.

While politicians may shudder at losing our rating's badge of honour, financial markets merely yawn. The silence was deafening when Standard and Poor's recently stated that there was:

> a one-in-three chance that we could lower the rating (for Australia) within the next two years if

we believe that parliament is unlikely to legislate savings or revenue measures sufficient for the general government sector budget deficit to narrow materially and to be in a balanced position by the early 2020s.

Following the S&P announcement, traders hardly batted an eyelid. In contrast, the tabloid media did its best to whip the populace into a frenzy. For my money, the most sensible and accurate headline was by *Bloomberg Markets*: "Worrying About Aussie AAA Is So 1980s as Economy Craves Stimulus".

Bloomberg's position regarding a ratings downgrade accords with my own. As I outlined in a recent post, *Austerity delusion*, Australia currently needs more sovereign debt, not less. We have a $500 billion backlog of infrastructure which needs to be funded via a fiscal stimulus.

The *Bloomberg* article noted that Australia has "large infrastructure needs" and that our "obsession over the rating is a misplaced concern". This is why the Australian government should be locking in long-term finance for infrastructure investment that will benefit current and future generations.

Given the prevailing rock-bottom rates at which the government can borrow, a fiscal stimulus is much more important than trying to maintain a rolled gold rating. Ironically, well-targeted fiscal spending can actually help reduce long-term government debt.

As to the claim that a ratings downgrade would increase the government's borrowing costs, history shows that this does not always happen. In reality, the loss of the AAA rating would have almost no effect on our economy. As noted by one economic commentator:

> In theory, a lower credit rating should lead to borrowers demanding a higher return for the risk they're taking. In the case of Australia however, since all its debt is denominated in Australian dollars which it is able to print, it can never technically default. This means Australia's borrowing costs are determined by expectations of where the Reserve Bank will set the cash rate. Other governments that have lost their AAA ratings such as the US and Japan have actually seen their borrowing costs fall because investors have assumed their central banks would hold official interest rates lower.

It is also claimed that higher borrowing costs would be imposed on our major banks because of a lower credit rating. However, the consensus is that the Reserve Bank of Australia (RBA) could adjust interest rates to offset any change. This would likely lead to a welcome fall in the Australian dollar.

The irony of this is not lost upon another economic commentator:

> The political obsession with credit ratings is reminiscent of the way nations once viewed their currency. Not so long ago, global leaders, including Australia's, openly boasted that a strong currency was a sign of economic strength. A weakening currency was a sure-fire

way to lose an election. Speak to any of them now and they will outline their latest cunning plan to undermine the value of their currencies in order to rejuvenate industry.

One of the reasons that the global economy is in a mess is because rating agencies did not do their jobs diligently. The countries they now sit in judgment on had to spend billions propping up their banking systems as a result of the Global Financial Crisis (GFC).

One of the causes of the GFC, of course, was the top ratings given to mortgage-backed securities by the rating agencies. As we all painfully know, these ratings misrepresented the risks associated with mortgage related securities which ultimately turned out to be worthless.

Given their track record, I find it a bit rich that the rating agencies get to judge the world. Talk about the pot calling the kettle black!

POSTING DATE │ 12 SEPTEMBER 2016

DEFLATIONrisk

It has long been my contention that slow drivers can potentially be more hazardous than fast drivers. Following this same reasoning, I believe that deflation (falling prices) can cause more harm to an economy than inflation (rising prices). As counter-intuitive as it sounds, the availability of cheaper goods because of falling prices is nothing to cheer about.

Deflation is a destructive force. It was present throughout most of the Great Depression and made a comeback in many parts of the world post-GFC. Now it has arrived on our shores and was the main driver of the recent Reserve Bank of Australia (RBA) decision to lower the cash rate. Price gains in Australia are below 2 per cent which is less than the RBA's target inflation band of 2–3 per cent.

It's a positive thing when the price of one item – like petrol – falls, as it allows us to spend more on other things. But when prices tumble across the board, the economy is in trouble. In anticipation of further falls, individuals and businesses change their normal consumption behaviour. They postpone purchases while waiting for lower prices and this causes demand to plummet.

Paradoxically, lower prices come at a high price. The belief that goods bought tomorrow will be cheaper than goods bought today chokes consumption. To quote Investopedia: "Why would you spend a dollar today when the expectation is that it could buy effectively more stuff tomorrow? And why spend tomorrow when things may be even cheaper in a week's time?"

The result of this downward demand spiral is a reduction in corporate profits, stagnation in wages and a contraction in the labour force. Workers who are laid off join the ranks of the unemployed. This, in turn, results in lower demand for products as out-of-work consumers can't afford more purchases. The result is a further decline in demand and so a vicious cycle begins.

Those who are lucky enough to retain their jobs after company cost-cutting purges typically experience a fall in real wages. Overtime evaporates due to less demand for the products being made. With reduced incomes, people have less money in their pockets even if each dollar can buy slightly more. So the vicious cycle accelerates.

Delaying purchases hampers the whole economic cycle, which is why central banks use monetary policy to stimulate an economy. Falling rates make borrowing more attractive and saving less attractive. Both factors – in theory – are supposed to boost consumer spending and business investment and this assists in kick-starting an economic recovery.

In practice, however, this has not happened post-GFC. Inflation has remained weak or flat-lined in many countries despite the presence of record low interest rates. Even negative rates have not increased demand and perked up prices. We are witnessing a dangerous phenomenon where weak inflation begets lower interest rates, which begets even lower inflation and so on.

It's clear that monetary policy alone is struggling to break the vicious cycle of falling prices. This is why governments must mobilise fiscal policy to do some of the heavy lifting. Nation-states need to boost aggregate demand by spending more on infrastructure. Australia currently has a $500 billion infrastructure backlog which can be reduced with an expansionary fiscal policy.

Now is not the time for austerity measures which reduce government spending. As world-renowned economist and Nobel laureate Paul Krugman has often observed, government finances are not like personal finances, for multiple reasons. One of them is the huge payback that social investments can deliver.

With Australian government bond yields at record lows, now is the time for the federal government to be borrowing more. Currently, the 10-year bond rate is just 2.29 per cent (lower than during the 1930s depression!). That's the interest we would pay for 10 years even if the bond yield goes up during that period.

We Aussies – to my frustration – have an irrational and emotive attitude to government debt, even though we have one of the world's lowest debt-to-GDP ratios. Yet as Professor Krugman pointed out when he was in Australia, there has never been a better time for governments (including Australia's) to borrow to fund necessary infrastructure.

Post-GFC, Krugman has repeatedly argued that governments around the world should adopt the Keynesian approach and accelerate spending to boost growth. In a seminal paper Krugman authored last year – *The Austerity Delusion* – he noted that "it's foolish and destructive to worry about deficits when borrowing is very cheap and the funds you borrow would otherwise go to waste".

It's a real shame that his message has fallen on deaf ears in Australia.

POSTING DATE │ 30 MAY 2016

ECONOMICpuzzle

Solving a puzzle is meant to be challenging. But when that puzzle is a Rubik's cube, with 43 quintillion possible combinations (that's 18 zeros), the task is near impossible. Players twist and turn the multicoloured cube's corners, edges and centre in an attempt to display one single colour on each of the six sides. Most discover that it's an unattainable goal as moving one piece to achieve colour alignment scrambles the opposite face.

Just like a Rubik's cube, there are many moving parts to an economy and each is a critical piece within a connected puzzle. We expect policymakers to shift the pieces to solve the economic puzzles we face. But the variables typically come together in a unique and different way each time. Also, a policy change in one area can lead to unintended repercussions elsewhere. The result is that solving one problem often creates other problems.

This is why policymakers require thinking that grasps the big picture, including the interrelationships among the full range of causal factors underlying them. We live in a Rubik's cube world where everything is intricately intertwined (e.g. climate change). Solving the Rubik's cube of falling productivity, economic inequality, budget deficits, trade imbalances and housing affordability, to name just a few matters, is easier said than done.

All economies face issues and governments intervene in an attempt to maintain economic stability and improve living standards. Major policy areas – like monetary and fiscal policies – must work in sync to produce optimal outcomes. But sometimes the issues are so complicated – as was the case with the Global Financial Crisis (GFC) – that economists, politicians and consumers struggle to understand the multiple dimensions.

The GFC was triggered by a housing bubble in the US which quickly fragmented political, economic and social landscapes around the world. The ensuing financial meltdown brought the free market to the precipice. The GFC starkly reminded us that national economies are linked umbilically in a globalised world. No country was able to decouple and escape the disruption to credit markets.

To avoid systemic collapse, extreme capitalism gave way to extreme intervention. The unfettered excesses of High Street were replaced by frantic spending programs for Main Street. Governments and central banks acted in unison, unveiling remarkable fiscal and monetary policy responses. Multi-billion-dollar stimulus packages and aggressive interest rate cuts were used to stimulate demand.

But the responses to the GFC were not identical. Some countries and economic regions understandably twisted the Rubik's cube to produce bespoke policy actions to shore up their national economy and local financial sector. Most major developed economies fell into recession and authorities deployed multi-pronged rescue plans. Some experimented with quantitative easing while others introduced zero interest rates.

In Australia, the Rudd Government pumped $10.4 billion into the pockets of Australian consumers. That fiscal stimulus package was based on Keynesian economics. British economist John Maynard Keynes believed that in a downturn, fiscal policy should be used to stimulate the economy. The cash transfer to low and middle-income Australians was designed to reduce the risk of a recession due to a phenomenon called the paradox of thrift.

This paradox describes the dilemma we face when times are tight. During a recession, we are encouraged to spend to keep the economy going. But our natural tendency is to save, and this triggers a cause-and-effect spiral to decreased economic activity.

The ride to recession begins when we all start saving our money and this reduces consumer spending. This, in turn, causes aggregate demand to fall and this, in turn again, results in a decline in total income. And when income falls, people have less to spend. So as counter-intuitive as it sounds, savings by individuals make us collectively poor.

The paradox of thrift is akin to a Rubik's cube as saving might appear beneficial at an individual level but it's actually detrimental to the population overall. One person's spending is another person's income. Yet again, changing one side of the cube alters the look of other sides.

An economy is as complicated as a Rubik's cube. This is why the GFC was a humbling experience for economic forecasters. As noted by one commentator: "An entire field of experts dedicated to studying the behaviour of markets failed to anticipate what may prove to be the biggest economic collapse of our lifetime".

While there needs to be a major rethink of economic tools and techniques, it's unreasonable to expect economists to be fortune tellers. In the words of celebrated economist John Kenneth Galbraith: "There are two kinds of economists – those who don't know the future and those who don't know they don't know".

POSTING DATE │ 17 OCTOBER 2016

SCALEdiseconomies

Modern society would have us believe that bigger is better. Today, our homes are bigger, our cars are bigger, our televisions are bigger and just about everything else we have is bigger. Moreover, our cities are replete with taller buildings, mega malls and busier airports – the world is on steroids!

Business too appears focussed on one outcome – the largest market share. Growth has long been the key imperative in business and economics. Growth strategies that increase scale are lauded. Indeed, they are considered best practice and are to be emulated by others.

But with size comes the challenges of diseconomies of scale. Larger companies are typically bureaucratic, inflexible and slow to react to changes. In contrast, newer firms constantly enter markets and take market share from established giants as they (smaller firms) are more agile and therefore better able to adapt to changing consumer needs.

Size also creates inefficiencies when it comes to decision-making. Hampered by their mass, big companies are not naturally nimble and innovative. The rigid organisational structures necessary to manage corporate behemoths inhibit the fluidity required to become the next Facebook or Apple.

In service industries, bigger firms often find it difficult to provide a high level of personal service. My wife and I have experienced this in the travel industry. We invariably find that smaller boutique hotels offer a far more intimate and caring standard of service than larger hotel chains.

Similarly, I still lament the closure of my neighbourhood hardware store which fell victim to the big brand players. Whereas I used to be warmly greeted by the local hardware store owner, I must now deal with an inexperienced young "concierge" at a mega-outlet who sends me off to some faraway aisle.

The Australian Superannuation Industry also espouses the big is better mantra. The prevailing wisdom of scale posits that bigger superannuation funds are cheaper for members. However, a 2012 working paper prepared for the Australian Prudential Regulation Authority (APRA) found that fund size does not have an overall positive impact on the performance of retail superannuation funds.

In a 2016 paper, *The myth of economies of scale: bigger is not necessarily better for super funds*, academic Dr Rob Nicholls also examined the claim that larger funds have an advantage in economies of scale over smaller funds. Specifically, he set out to test the belief that:

> superannuation funds with more assets under management … benefit from economies of scale, because the costs of running a superannuation fund are largely fixed and do not change much, whether you are managing assets of A$500 million or $50 billion.

For years, we have been told that superannuation funds with more assets under management spend proportionally less on administration and overheads. This allegedly allows them to make more competitive returns and supposedly gives them an edge in the marketplace.

However, Dr Nicholls' findings were in stark contrast to the prevailing wisdom about the superannuation sector and indeed the classic economic theory of economies of scale. He noted:

> Not only do the biggest funds have no discernible efficiency advantage over the much smaller mid-sized funds, but there are some positively tiny funds which are just as efficient as some of the very largest.

In banking, there is the problem of too big to fail or – as some would say – too big to save. Since the Global Financial Crisis (GFC), there have been waves of calls to break up massive banks around the world that are systemically too important to fail. Chopping them up into manageable bits is seen as a solution.

However, this "solution" fails to recognise that all banks – big and small – are interconnected in their activities. Banks are financially exposed to one another through the payments system and other types of activities such as loans and derivatives thereby creating interbank liabilities.

These balance sheet linkages between financial institutions mean that they are "too interconnected to fail". This is why bank failures create a domino effect. Financial difficulties at one bank can quickly spill over to other banks or the financial system as a whole, resulting in a wave of distressed institutions.

This is what occurred in Spain during the GFC. Many of Spain's small savings banks stumbled and collectively caused as much disruption as one distressed big bank. So troubled small banks can create a level of damage equal to a troubled big bank.

Please let me conclude this post by underscoring that bigger is not always bad, but it's not always better. Bigger is better for some things but not everything. What is clear is that you need to jump through more hoops to get things done in a big business whereas small businesses are largely free from inefficient red tape.

In both my professional and personal lives, I believe that the quality of what you do is far more important than the quantity. This is why I have enormous respect for small and medium sized enterprises (SMEs). In Australia, the SME sector is the largest employer in the country providing jobs for almost 60 per cent of the workforce.

Around the world, SMEs are the bedrock of most domestic economies. They account for 60 to 70 per cent of jobs in most OECD countries and are essential, therefore, to a prosperous economy. Increasingly, SMEs are creating a digital presence to combine local strength with global reach.

It's true that big business dominates the business pages while small business receives a miniscule amount of media attention. But small business is responsible for a lot of big thinking. And remember, every big business started as a small business.

POSTING DATE | 2 APRIL 2018

HOUSINGaffordability

Some nuts are hard to crack. In Australia, housing affordability is one of them. As each year passes, property becomes dearer relative to our incomes. Home ownership – the Great Australia Dream – is becoming out of reach for an increasing number of Aussies.

According to a recent survey undertaken by Demographia, Australia has the third most expensive housing market in the world. Hong Kong took first spot with New Zealand coming in second. The survey compared average home prices to median income in 406 cities in nine countries.

Houses that cost more than five times the median income are considered "severely unaffordable". Five of the 29 cities that carry this severe rating by Demographia are in Australia. Housing in our capital cities is among the least affordable in the world.

Sydney's housing is 12.2 times the median income while Melbourne's is 9.5 times the median income. Adelaide, Brisbane and Perth were also ranked "severely unaffordable", coming in at 6.6, 6.2 and 6.1 times the median income respectively.

On the rating scale used by Demographia, a ratio at or below three times median earnings is considered "affordable". This means Sydney is four times what it should be, making it the second most unaffordable housing location on the planet.

Sydney ranks above cities traditionally associated with expensive real estate like London, New York, San Francisco and Los Angeles. Sydney's property prices have gone through the roof over recent years, driving the median house price to a record $1,123,991.

The survey results paint a dire picture for low to middle income Australian families. Decent housing in our major cities is notoriously unaffordable. Demographia rates only four Australian regions as "affordable" – Karratha, Port Headland, Kalgoorlie and Gladstone.

So, who is to blame for this housing affordability crisis? Well, the list of alleged culprits recklessly driving up home prices includes wealthy baby boomers, greedy property investors, rogue offshore buyers, aggressive property lenders and apathetic policy makers.

More specifically, the federal government is accused of fuelling prices by allowing negative gearing. State governments are said to add to the problem by releasing insufficient supplies of land. And local councils are chastised for being too slow to approve new residential developments.

The Reserve Bank of Australia does not escape criticism with its ultra-low interest rate settings seen by some as misguided. And, of course, no national debate would be complete without pointing the finger at rising immigration for our woes, even if it's deceitful.

But isn't the blame-game truth a lot closer to home? We Aussies love to borrow. As I pointed out in last week's post, *Excessive consumerism*, Australian households are the most indebted in the world. We take on super-sized mortgages so that we can outbid each other at auctions.

Like the board game Monopoly, Aussies love to throw the dice on property.

We buy, we sell and we speculate in our efforts to climb the property ladder. The housing sector is the single biggest asset class in Australia. The total value of housing across the country is $6.4 trillion – equivalent to almost four times annual GDP. Investors own almost one-third of this housing stock and account for nearly half of the demand for new mortgages.

The brutal reality is that few people really want house prices to drop as most of our wealth is stored in housing. As money became progressively cheaper post-GFC, many Australians borrowed more and this increased indebtedness has been the major driver of rising house prices. In Sydney and Melbourne, average property prices have risen by about 90 per cent in the past decade, matching the increase in debt-servicing power.

It's part of our national psyche to want your own little piece of Australia. We have one of the highest rates of home ownership in the world thanks to our love affair with bricks and mortar. Housing not only provides us with shelter but a stable and permanent return on our money.

For millennial Aussies, the dream of a place to call home has become a nightmare. While their parents were able to buy a home, which sat on the proverbial quarter-acre suburban block, many younger Aussies are struggling even to buy a bed-sitter apartment.

We are becoming a nation of haves and have-nots and housing is the dividing line. Home owners are vastly wealthier than renters. With younger people and lower income families seemingly locked out of the housing market, one thing is clear: There is no one-size-fits-all solution to the home affordability crunch.

POSTING DATE | 20 MARCH 2017

HOUSINGboom

In Australia, home ownership is becoming increasingly unattainable. Younger people and low-income families in particular view the property market as impenetrable. These two demographic groups have been severely impacted by surging home values and have been priced out of the market. Affordable housing is now a political hot potato.

With home ownership in Australia at a 60-year low, the race is on to fix the problem. The good news is that there is no shortage of experts with a potential solution. The bad news is that housing affordability is a multifaceted and emotive issue with numerous players and competing interests. It is not a single problem but the accumulation of many problems.

That's why just building more homes will not solve the housing crisis because it's much more than a supply issue. Yet that silver bullet solution – build, build, build – has been proffered by many supposed experts. Despite a record five-year boom in housing supply, home values have continued to sky-rocket across many parts of the country.

Housing markets are complex systems which challenge conventional economic wisdom. According to economic theory, if we increase the supply of houses they will become more affordable. Yet in greater Sydney, house prices have risen by 40 per cent since 2011 while dwelling completions have ballooned by 85 per cent.

The theory of supply and demand does not accurately explain the workings of the housing market – here's why.

When the price of, say, apples rises, people will either buy fewer apples or switch to a cheaper fruit. But with housing, a rise in price actually stimulates demand. Professor Peter Phibbs from Sydney University explains the driver of this apparent perverse behaviour as follows:

> The key difference with housing is that it's an asset market, so when prices go up, particularly in the investor segment, people become more attracted to the product. You don't see the same change in demand as a result of price changes – you in fact get the opposite effect because it's a durable investment good. People aren't as interested in buying when the prices (of homes) are flat or going down – it's when prices go up that people want to get into the market.

So, increases to housing supply have only a limited impact on prices. Expanded stock simply draws more demand from investors eager to capitalise upon buoyant market conditions. In the words of Professor Phibbs "to tout new housing production as the only policy lever without examining the question of demand is clearly an ineffective policy position".

Professor Phibbs underscores the dangers of focussing exclusively on supply side solutions to housing affordability with examples from other countries:

> Looking around the world, rapid increases in housing supply are associated with price increases (the US, Spain, Ireland) not decreases. Ireland, for example, which has about the same population as Sydney, tripled its housing

production from around 30,000 homes a year in the mid-1990s to a peak of 89,000 dwellings in 2006, but house prices increased too – by 350 per cent across the country, and more than 400 per cent in Dublin.

The two groups most blamed for pushing up property prices across Australia during this current boom are up-graders and investors – certainly not first-time buyers. The surge in house prices that they have driven has moved in step with a surge in household debt. The amount households are borrowing for housing is getting more disproportionate to their pay packet.

As I opined in a recent post, *Excessive consumerism*, Australians love to borrow to buy property and are in hock to the tune of more than $1.4 trillion on housing. Post-GFC, cheap money created what some say is a credit-fuelled housing bubble. Those who believe the market will crash (I'm not one of them) argue that Australians are displaying the same "irrational exuberance" that Americans did prior to their housing crash.

Determining which demographic group is most behind this self-perpetuating exuberance is akin to pointing the finger of blame. But people love scapegoats and many Aussies have recently taken to blaming foreign buyers even though the data does not support this assertion. Chinese nationals own only a small portion of Australia's housing stock.

What the data from the Australian Bureau of Statistics does tell us is that investors currently make up 40 per cent of all housing finance commitments, up from only 28 per cent in 1996. So, as is often the case, the real culprit for rising property values is much closer to home. Mum and dad landlords have been criticised for elbowing first home buyers out of the market by buying up entry-level homes.

Moreover, our tax system plays an unusual role in encouraging individual investment in residential real estate. Perhaps it's time for politicians to consider trimming back the generous tax concessions on investor housing – negative gearing and capital gains discount. Of course, the electorate won't like that, so it won't happen.

Meanwhile, the wheels on the bus go round and round ...

POSTING DATE │ 3 APRIL 2017

HOUSINGbubble

There are some words that you are not supposed to mention for fear of causing panic. When it comes to the housing market, one such word is "bubble". Yet this emotive label is being bandied around by all and sundry – and it's getting attention and grabbing headlines.

History shows that market bubbles are never crystal clear at the time. If that were the case, runaway price increases would stop. It's only when asset prices reach dizzy heights that a critical mass of people – economists included – agree that they are overpriced and due for a major correction.

As noted by economic researcher Timo Henckel from the Australian National University:

> Economists disagree on how to define a bubble, or even whether bubbles exist. Intuitively, a bubble (and this applies to any asset, not just real estate) exists when the price of an asset is over-inflated relative to some benchmark. And here's the rub: no one can agree on what that benchmark should be.

Consequently, no one can conclusively claim that Australia currently faces a housing bubble. Nonetheless, debate rages whether the Sydney and Melbourne property markets are in a bubble which is on the brink of popping. If you believe the naysayers, the imminent price correction will be devastating.

In the cold light of day, dire warnings of a housing market bloodbath do not reflect history. Australia's housing markets are characterised by orderly growth and correction phases. There has never been a collapse of Australian capital property values in modern times.

Regardless, the media is replete with predictions of a hard landing for residential property. While the scaremongers continue to attract most of the air time by talking up the possibility of a crash, other commentators with more measured assessments should also be heard.

To this end, S&P believes that the east coast residential property boom will "unwind in an orderly manner, as has generally been the case over past property cycles". The ratings agency added that a "sharp fall in property prices remains unlikely in the next two years".

Similarly, a recently released home values report by CoreLogic-Moody's forecasts that Sydney and Melbourne house prices will fall marginally between 2018 and 2020. During this period, Sydney home prices will decline by 1.4 per cent in 2018 and by another 0.9 per cent in 2019.

Sydney prices will rise again after 2020 but nowhere near the double-digit growth of the past four years. "Although we do not expect a steep decline in prices, Sydney's property market will likely stagnate through to 2020 as interest rates begin to normalise," the CoreLogic-Moody's report says.

Louis Christopher, MD of SQM Research and arguably one of the country's most accurate forecasters of house price growth, recently stated that "the last downturn in Sydney was in 2004, where the market did correct a little bit that year and then stayed flat for an extended period of time".

According to Mr Christopher, ongoing strong population growth in Sydney and Melbourne will continue to drive underlying demand for housing and should act as a buffer against any major correction. But not everyone is as sanguine about the future value of housing.

Dr John Hewson recently declared that Australia has a property bubble. The boss of the Australian Securities & Investments Commission (ASIC), Greg Medcraft, supports this view. Two years ago, Commonwealth Treasury secretary John Fraser also declared a bubble in parts of the Sydney and Melbourne markets.

But at a banking conference in March, Australian Prudential Regulation Authority (APRA) boss Wayne Byres refused to utter the word "bubble", instead opting for the "B-word" reference. "I don't use the B-word. I refuse to use the B-word," said Byres. "It implies a binary, that's too simplistic".

Likewise, the Reserve Bank of Australia (RBA) refrained from using the B-word in the minutes of its last board meeting, preferring to say there is a "build-up of risks". That accords with the language of the big banks and is a narrative that I believe more accurately reflects the state of the housing market.

From a risk perspective, there are two macro-triggers that could give rise to a home price collapse. Widespread job losses would be one, but there is no talk of that. A rapid rise in rates would be another, but with low inflation and low growth, the RBA will want to raise rates gently to cushion households.

Monetary policy is a blunt tool with interest rate rises affecting both housing and business lending. So, the RBA is unlikely to push rates higher just to quell housing market exuberance. Doing so could push the Australian dollar higher, plus reduce much-needed stimulus to many sectors of the economy.

This is why the RBA has been working in concert with other regulators to assess and contain housing market risks. APRA and ASIC have been able to target segments of the market – such as investor and interest only loans – thereby negating the need for RBA intervention via interest rates hikes.

In 2015, the RBA stress tested the financial resilience of Australian households to "macroeconomic shock". The RBA concluded that even if house prices plunged by a quarter, likely losses for banks would only be "limited" because most of the debt is held by higher income earners.

When all is said and done, predicting the demise of the Australian housing market has become a sport. For fifty years, the pundits have been calling a crash. However, my considered opinion is that – in the absence of either a recession or much higher interest rates – a property crash is highly unlikely.

POSTING DATE | 1 MAY 2017

STOCKindices

America has the S&P 500 Index. Japan has the Nikkei 225 Index. Australia has the ASX 200. The UK has the FTSE 100. And Germany has the DAX 30 Index. Stock exchanges around the world calculate and publish a range of indices to track the performance of a specific "basket" of stocks traded on their stock exchanges.

A stock index is a measurement of the value of a section of the stock market, not the entire market. A group of similar stocks are grouped together to form an index. This classification may be based on industry lines, company size, market capitalisation or some other basis. There are indices for almost every sector of the economy and stock market.

At the end of each day's trading, news reports tell us whether the market fell or rose. But that does not mean that every single stock moved in unison. The term "market" means an index. On any given day, individual stocks can and do move in the opposite direction to the market index as the market is not a single entity.

National indices are composed of the stocks of companies listed on a country's stock exchanges. The Dow Jones Industrial Average is arguably the world's best known and most widely-followed stock market index. It consists of 30 large, publicly traded blue chip firms in the US and includes financial services companies, computer companies and retail companies.

Around the world, broad market indices – like the Hang Seng Index – attract the most media coverage. But there is a host of more narrow indices that measure the performance of different groups of shares. The NYSE Arca Tech 100 is a specialised index for US technology-related stocks while the ASX Small Ordinaries Index is a key benchmark for small-cap investment in Australia.

Market indices record the ups and downs of investing and function as statistical gauges of the market's activities. Investors use indices to track the performance of the broader market or a discrete segment. Indices reflect the sentiments of investors and the direction of the market. In share market parlance (as explained by Investopedia) there are two types of markets – bull and bear.

> The use of "bull" and "bear" to describe markets comes from the way the animals attack their opponents. A bull thrusts its horns up into the air, while a bear swipes its paws downward. These actions are metaphors for the movement of a market. If the trend is up, it's a bull market. If the trend is down, it's a bear market.

Bull markets are characterised by optimism, investor confidence and expectations that strong results should continue. In contrast, bear markets are characterised by falling prices and are typically shrouded in pessimism. Bull and bear markets typically coincide with the economic cycle. To again quote Investopedia:

> The onset of a bull market is often a leading indicator of economic expansion. Because public sentiment about future economic conditions drives stock prices, the market frequently rises even before broader economic

measures, such as GDP growth, begin to tick up. Likewise, bear markets usually set in before economic contraction takes hold. A look back (at most recessions) reveals a falling stock market several months ahead of GDP decline.

Investor sentiment is reflected in performance indices because the market is determined by the attitude of investors. Indeed, stock market performance and investor psychology are mutually dependent. We have long known that most investors are emotional. Thus, the old Wall Street saying that the market is driven by just two emotions: fear and greed.

The Global Financial Crisis (GFC) revealed the devastating impact that human emotions have on markets. During the GFC, investor confidence plummeted causing a stampede for the exit door. The human species was convinced it faced financial Armageddon and this supposedly intelligent herd animal behaved like one of Pavlov's dogs – the market rings the bell and hysteria starts.

The GFC equity market panic demonstrated that markets are not populated by rational decision makers. One can only wonder – if we had acted more rationally – whether we could have avoided or mitigated the market death spiral. Ironically, the panic sell-off was partly fuelled by market indices which became self-fulfilling prophecies that put markets in a steep slide.

Indices are the pulse of equity markets, but they are not perfect. They provide snapshots of market movements but not always the full picture. In reality, stock prices are governed by expectations which may or may not be rational. If an index is down, many investors will automatically adopt a bearish outlook. In contrast, if an index is up, sentiments will invariably turn bullish.

We find it easy to rely on indices and the 30-second trend analysis that they provide. While index sound-bites are certainly helpful, they should never replace sound reasoning. Sometimes it's best to ignore the herd and stay the course.

POSTING DATE │ 15 MAY 2017

CURRENCYexchange

Australians are increasingly travelling overseas, and money is an essential item on the packing list. But how far your holiday dollar goes depends upon your destination. The Australian dollar is stronger against some currencies and weaker against others – it all depends on the exchange rate.

An exchange rate represents the relative price of two currencies. It is the value of one currency expressed in another currency. Put another way, an exchange rate is the purchasing power of one currency against another or the ratio by which one currency is converted into another.

There are two ways that you can approach currency conversion. You can start with the Australian dollars you have (let's say $2,000) and convert those to a foreign currency. Or you can start with the foreign currency you need (let's say €500) and convert that amount to Australian dollars.

To convert Australian dollars into overseas money you must always *multiply* the Australian dollar amount by the exchange rate. Conversely, to convert foreign currency into Australian dollars you must always *divide* the other currency by our exchange rate.

There are two categories of exchange rates – *buy* and *sell* – and these must be viewed from the perspective of your bank. If you buy US dollars from your bank, it will use the *sell* rate as it is selling you foreign currency. It follows, therefore, that if you sell US dollars to your bank, it will use the *buy* rate as it is buying foreign currency.

The exchange rates that you see on the nightly news are the rates that banks charge each other when trading significant amounts of foreign currency. These wholesale rates are not offered to tourists when buying small amounts of currency – travellers receive less attractive retail exchange rates.

Okay, let's put all this theory together with some practical examples. Let's say you want to buy USD using AUD100. The bank's selling rate for this transaction is 0.71. So, you multiply the AUD100 by 0.71 to get USD71. In other words, one Australian dollar buys 71 US cents.

Now let's look at this example the other way around. This time we want to sell USD100 in exchange for AUD. The bank's buying rate for this transaction is 0.74. So, you divide the USD100 by 0.74 to get AUD135. In other words, one US dollar buys 1.35 Australian dollars.

Nations around the world use one of two systems to determine the exchange rate of their currency – either a fixed or a floating regime. A fixed system is typically used by smaller countries to stabilise the value of their currency. A floating system is used by most of the world's larger nations.

A fixed exchange rate is fixed by the government and not determined by market forces. Under such a system, a country will normally peg its currency to a major currency. This means the value of the currency is always worth exactly the same amount of another, as its value is fixed in a predetermined ratio to a more stable and prevalent currency like the greenback or euro.

In contrast, a country with a floating exchange rate allows the value of its currency to be determined by the forces of supply and demand. The currency fluctuates freely according to trading in the foreign exchange market. The value of the currency isn't related to any other and is determined by how much people will pay for it on the foreign exchange market.

The foreign exchange market (also known as forex) is the largest financial market in the world. The Bank for International Settlements undertakes a triennial survey of the size of the global foreign exchange market. As at April 2013, the average daily turnover was a staggering $5.3 trillion. To put this into perspective, this averages out to be $220 billion per hour.

This volume of trading certainly overshadows the spending money I will be taking on my next overseas holiday!

POSTING DATE | 6 JUNE 2016

RENTALyields

Property is an increasingly popular way for Australians to invest. Over 1.7 million Aussies (or 7.9 per cent of the population) own an investment property. As an asset class, an investment in bricks and mortar is not considered to be as safe as cash, but it's less risky than equities. Regardless, landlords want an acceptable return on their investment.

When it comes to real estate, the return on investment takes the form of a rental yield. This is a measure of the rental income as a percentage of the property's value. It can be calculated as a gross percentage (before expenses are deducted) or as a net percentage (with expenses and purchasing costs included).

Let's crunch some numbers to see how it works in practice. Let's say that you buy an apartment for $800,000 and charge $800 per week in rent. This generates an annual rental income of $41,600. Dividing the $41,600 income by $800,000 x 100 produces a gross rental yield of 5.2 per cent.

While the gross rental yield only requires two figures, calculating the net rental yield entails many more factors. There are myriad fees and expenses associated with owning a property. Most of these costs are variable – and some will be known, while others need to be estimated. So, net rental is harder to calculate but produces a more accurate yield.

Regardless of the yield methodology used, soaring property prices cause yields to plummet if rents can't keep pace with the growth. In the example above, if the value of the property jumped from $800,000 to $1m and the rental income remained unchanged at $800 per week, the yield would drop to 4.2 per cent.

This is why the recent house price boom in the Sydney and Melbourne markets pushed rental yields to near record lows. Gross rental yields for houses in Australia's two biggest capital cities are now below 3 per cent. Paradoxically, the two cities with the greatest property investment activity in Australia are also the cities with the lowest rental yields.

Unless investors are banking on future capital gains or a large rise in rents, further investments in Sydney and Melbourne should be approached with caution. Over recent weeks, house price growth in Sydney and Melbourne has moderated, so future capital gains on investment properties will be more subdued.

Chasing capital growth ahead of rental yields is a legitimate investment strategy. It does, however, raise the age-old debate about which strategy is better. In a perfect world, the best possible investment outcome for a property investor is a combination of decent house price growth and rising rental income.

But the world is not perfect, so choices must be made. Over recent years, property investors have been excessively eager to buy at prices that imply they are betting only on future capital gains rather than meaningful rental returns.

Where and what to buy are also important investment decisions. Savvy investors know that apartments tend to offer higher rental returns than detached houses because the initial investment (purchase price) is lower.

Also, it is invariably better to buy in a suburb with affordable rents rather than a blue chip suburb with sky high rents that few can afford. Those who do buy in an expensive suburb need to be confident that the rental demand in the area is strong enough to offset the higher costs of ownership.

To state the blindingly obvious, a vacant investment property does not produce income and there will be times when a property is not tenanted. But this must be the exception, not the rule. Landlords must keep a close eye on vacancy rates which compare the demand from renters with how much rental supply is actually available to them.

The Australian Securities & Investments Commission (ASIC) has some useful information on its website about buying an investment property. Among other things, ASIC advises the following:

- *Familiar markets* – Consider buying an investment property in an area you are familiar with as it will take you less time to research. Check recent sale prices in the area to give you an idea of what you can expect to pay for local properties.

- *Growth suburbs* – Look for areas where high growth is expected, where there is potential for capital gains.

- *Rental yield* – Look for areas where rents are high compared to the property value.

- *Low vacancy rates* – Find out about the vacancy rates in the neighbourhood. A high vacancy rate may indicate a less desirable area, which could make it harder to rent the property out or sell it in the future.

- *Planning* – Find out about proposed changes in the suburb that may affect future property prices. Things like new developments or zoning changes can affect the future value of a property.

Property investment is not rocket science – anyone can do it. With a bit of research and a level head, you too can find an investment property to suit your budget. Finally, it is important to remember that property is a long-term investment – it's not a quick fix to financial problems.

POSTING DATE │ 10 JULY 2017

EXPENSIVEcities

Good news – Sydney is not the dearest city in the world in which to live. Nor is Melbourne. Flashy Monaco doesn't even rate a mention in the top 10 most expensive cities. Believe it or not, tiny Singapore comes out on top in the world rankings for 2017.

This year's *Worldwide Cost of Living Report*, carried out by *The Economist* Intelligence Unit, crowned Singapore as the world's most expensive city for the fourth year running. Singapore – the world's only island city-state – is 20 per cent more expensive than New York and 5 per cent pricier than Hong Kong, which lies in second place. Switzerland's banking capital, Zurich, occupies the third spot.

Tokyo lost its crown as the world's dearest city in 2012. This year, due to a strengthening yen, the Japanese capital climbed seven notches in the ranking to take fourth rung on the ladder. New York – which rose to seventh place in 2016 – slid to ninth place due to a slightly weakening greenback.

Europe had four cities in the top 10, with Geneva, Paris and Copenhagen joining Zurich. Both Sydney and Melbourne climbed six notches to take 14th and 15th spot respectively. The Brazilian cities of São Paulo and Rio de Janeiro have the unenviable honour of recording the fastest rising cost of living in the world, moving up 29 and 27 places respectively.

The study compared more than 400 individual prices across 160 goods and services in 133 cities around the world. It is primarily used by human resources managers to calculate compensation packages for expats and business travellers. Categories include food, clothing, household supplies, rent, utility bills, education and transportation.

Transportation includes the cost of owning a motor vehicle and this is largely why Singapore is the world's costliest city. Owning a car in Singapore is insanely expensive due to punitive government taxes. These are designed to keep private cars off the road and "force" Singaporeans to use public transport.

Before you can register a vehicle in Singapore, you must purchase (in an open bid process) a Certificate of Entitlement (COE) from the government. A COE gives you the right to own a vehicle for 10 years and they are currently priced around S$50,000. The government also enforces a Vehicle Quota System to limit the growth of the vehicle population.

Excuse my digression. Now back to the *Cost of Living Report* to look at how Britain fared. Living in London is the cheapest it has been in decades. So if you're planning a trip to the British capital, go now! The depreciation of the sterling post-Brexit helped pull London down the rankings to 24th spot, its lowest position in 20 years.

London is now the cheapest of the world's major global centres, with the cost of living falling behind that of New York, Paris and Tokyo. While London fell 18 places, Manchester's fall was even sharper. It recorded the steepest cost of living fall of any city in the world – 25 places to 51st spot. Relative prices in Manchester are now on par with Bangkok.

But Manchester is not the cheapest place in the word to live. That title belongs to Almaty in Kazakhstan. Not surprisingly, India has four of the least expensive cities – New Delhi, Mumbai, Bangalore and Chennai. If you're looking for the cheapest major city in Australia, then you should head to Perth. The Western Australian capital is 49th on the list of most expensive cities in the world.

Please allow me to end with a note of caution. Comparing the price of goods and services between countries is not a strict apples-to-apples comparison. There will typically be local variations in the quality of goods. The other factor to note is that all cities are compared using New York as a base city. But comparing apples to the Big Apple using US dollars can be somewhat academic.

Currency movements – both up and down – contribute to the rise and fall in the relative cost of living between cities and this can make a given city expensive for an expat or other foreigner. However, in one's home city – like Sydney – a dollar is still a dollar for Sydneysiders irrespective of what is happening beyond our shores regarding the value of the Aussie dollar.

So enjoy the survey, but take the results with a pinch of salt.

POSTING DATE | 22 MAY 2017

MASSIVElandowners

It's claimed that Queen Elizabeth II is the largest landowner on Earth. As head of the Commonwealth of Nations, she is technically the legal owner of 6.6 billion acres of terra firma. In reality, Her Majesty does not personally own all the land in her realms. Rather, it is owned by the millions of her subjects who hold title to a parcel of land, granted by the Crown.

Unlike Queen Elizabeth, other monarchs are huge landholders in their own right. Number one on this list is King Salman of Saudi Arabia who has absolute royal control over the 547 million acres of the oil-rich Kingdom of Saudi Arabia. Next is King Mohammed VI of Morocco who controls 175.6 million acres of land. King Vajiralongkorn of Thailand comes in third with 128 million acres under his crown.

Nation-states also control huge tracts of land. The Russian state tops this list with a direct ownership holding of 2.4 billion acres. It is closely followed by the Chinese state which claims all of China's land – about 2.3 billion acres. In third spot is the Federal Government of the United States, which owns about one-third of the land of the USA or 760 million acres.

Following nation-states and monarchies, the world's largest private landholding is right here in Australia. It's a collection of outback properties owned (until recently) by S. Kidman & Co. It comprises 10 working cattle stations and spans a whopping 27.2 million acres (11 million hectares). This is about three-quarters the size of England or an area equivalent in size to South Korea.

Unsurprisingly, the Catholic Church – with cathedrals, churches, convents and schools scattered throughout the globe – is also a very large landholder. But getting official figures on ecclesiastical real estate is virtually impossible. Vatican City, the smallest independent city-state in the world, sits on 110 acres of land. Beyond that, it's anyone's guess how many more millions of acres the church owns.

Another ubiquitous organisation is McDonalds and it has over 35,000 chain stores scattered around the world. The average McDonalds store sits on 1.15 acres, making the total about 40,000 acres. While it makes hamburgers, McDonalds has long been considered one of the world's biggest real estate companies. The company makes most of its money from the rent paid by its franchisees on the company-owned properties they lease.

Many business tycoons are also land barons and perhaps the most famous is Amazon founder Jeff Bezos. Bezos has invested some of his wealth into building a fabulous real estate portfolio. His largest parcel of land is his 290,000-acre ranch in Texas. The land is used by Blue Origin, the space exploration company owned by Bezos, to test fully reusable rockets.

In terms of land usage, food production (land used for both crops and livestock) takes up around 40 per cent of the Earth's land surface. This, according to one report, makes our planet "a gigantic farm, one occasionally broken up by cities, forests and the oceans". Clearly, it takes a lot of farmland to keep all seven billion of us humans fed!

The composition of farmland is slowly but surely changing. Small farmers are being squeezed out as mega-farms and plantations gobble up their land. Fertile agricultural land is being concentrated in the hands of fewer owners – typically corporations – that are gearing up to feed nine billion mouths by 2050. By this time, the population will not only be larger, but also more urban and richer. Food production, therefore, will need to increase by around 70 per cent.

Land sustains life and creates wealth and is the basis for most human activities on Earth. Agriculture, forestry, transport, industry, housing and other services use land as a natural and/or an economic resource. In classical economics, land is considered one of the three factors of production along with capital and labour.

Australia's love affair with land (real estate) is well known. More than 65 per cent of Australians own a home – one of the highest rates of home ownership in the world. The Australian housing sector is the nation's largest and arguably most important asset class.

Figures from the Australian Bureau of Statistics show that the total value of Australia's 9.8 million residential dwellings as at December 2016 was $6.4 trillion. This, according to RP Data, is almost three times larger than the size of our combined superannuation at $2.3 trillion, followed by listed stocks at $1.6 trillion. Residential land and dwellings account for over 52 per cent of Australia's total household wealth.

Historically, more fortunes have been made owning land than any other investment class. Land is a finite resource and some individuals have left a large footprint on it. The world's biggest landowners certainly have their feet planted firmly on the ground.

POSTING DATE │ 20 NOVEMBER 2017

FAITH-BASED investing

The ability to invest along religious lines is gaining momentum. Some people of faith are avoiding "sin stocks" in favour of spiritually responsible funds. Such Individuals want their investments to grow, but not at the expense of strongly held moral beliefs.

Special funds are available for Catholics, Protestants and Muslims who seek investments in companies that do not violate the tenets of their religion. These funds are a subset of socially responsible funds which consider both financial return and social good, i.e. investing with both the head and the heart.

The Ave Maria Funds in the US screen out businesses that promote or support activities contrary to the core moral teachings of the Catholic Church. The funds have a pro-family investment philosophy that shuns companies involved with abortion, contraception or embryonic stem cell research.

Another US fund that invokes biblical values is the Inspire Global Hope ETF. The fund believes that "good returns and good values are not mutually exclusive". It adopts a conservative evangelical approach to investing and excludes any company associated with gambling, alcohol or pornography.

Muslims who are strictly observant to Sharia law and want to invest "the Islamic way" may utilise the Amana Mutual Funds Trust. These funds evaluate a company's business activities to ascertain if what it does is permitted *(halal)* or not permitted *(haram)* under Islamic law.

To this end, the Amana Funds do not invest in the money market or most banks because collecting interest is against the religion's teachings. Other Sharia-compliant restrictions include a ban on investments in "unholy" stocks including alcohol, tobacco, weapons, pork and entertainment.

In Australia, the Catholic Superannuation Fund ranks as the nation's biggest religious-based financial services group. With more than $7 billion in funds under management and more than 70,000 members, Catholic Super is a signatory to the United Nations Principles of Responsible Investment.

Each religious group has a slightly different take on how to incorporate its values into investments. But they are united in their belief that economic success should never come at the expense of human dignity. Non-secular investors take pride from investing with a clear conscience.

Of course, faith-based investing still requires a leap of faith and this, it is claimed, is made easier when you can jump into stocks that reflect your religious creed. In a pragmatic sense, putting your money where your faith is demonstrates your biblical stewardship.

However, investing in sync with religious beliefs does not guarantee divine returns and, indeed, may even yield fewer loaves. For example, the loathsome tobacco industry has produced some of the best investment returns over many decades. Boycotting this sector, therefore, due to your virtues will cost you.

A feature article in the *Atlantic* magazine titled 'The Conscious Investor' opined that in a perfect world,

Socially Responsible Investing (SRI) should promote practices that improve life for everyone, not just those whose religious or personal beliefs lead them to value some products and services over others.

The article bemoaned that the main problem with eliminating "objectionable" companies is that "objection-able" is in the eye of the beholder:

> After tobacco, the next two industries on the list (of socially unredeemable industries) are alcohol and gambling; more than half of SRI mutual funds eliminate them. Alcohol and gambling certainly cause plenty of problems. Alcohol, especially, kills, maims, screws up families, and turns customers into addicts and occasionally into murderers … On the other hand, would you really want the winery that produces your favorite pinot noir to go bankrupt? The tens of millions of people who jet to Las Vegas each year might tell their pastors that the Luxor is evil, but it's hard to believe they (or their pastors) never intend to go back.

It's clear that meeting both monetary and moral objectives can be a challenge for the pious. But God and Mammon can go together assuming the devout are prepared to potentially sacrifice investment performance for the intrinsic reward of knowing that their investment choices can help make the world a better place.

POSTING DATE │ 19 JUNE 2017

OPENbanking

It's being heralded as the biggest change to banking since the advent of the Internet. Pundits claim that it will give power to the people by enabling them to digitally access and securely share their bank transaction data. This will empower customers to seek out better and cheaper financial products.

Open banking has the potential to revolutionise the way we manage our money. It will force banks to open their customer data to third-parties – via secure data sharing mechanisms called APIs. This will provide consumers with more choice on how they transact, save, borrow, lend and invest their money.

An API – Application Processing Interface – is a piece of software that allows different computer systems to connect. In the case of open banking, APIs will provide a standardised way for banks to store their data so that licensed third-parties can access it. Think of it like a single filing system for everyone to use. APIs will enable third-party developers to build helpful services and tools that customers can utilise.

Last year, the UK government announced its support for open banking. This followed a 2016 report prepared by the government's Competition and Markets Authority which concluded that "older and larger banks do not have to compete hard enough for customers' business, and smaller and newer banks find it difficult to grow. This means that many people are paying more than they should and are not benefiting from new services".

The Competition and Markets Authority recommended that all UK banks be required to implement open banking by early 2018, saying that it:

> will enable personal customers and small businesses to share their data securely with other banks and with third-parties, enabling them to manage their accounts with multiple providers through a single digital 'app', to take more control of their funds (for example to avoid overdraft charges and manage cashflow) and to compare products on the basis of their own requirements.

Australian lawmakers have been closely watching UK developments. In the May budget, Federal Treasurer Scott Morrison foreshadowed that the government would commission a review into the best way to set up an open banking regime in Australia. Announcing the review in July, Treasurer Morrison said:

> Greater consumer access to their own banking data and data on banking products will allow consumers to seek out products that better suit their circumstances, saving them money and allowing them to better achieve their financial goals. It will also create further opportunities for innovative business models to drive greater competition in banking and contribute to productivity growth.

If the Australian government gets its way, financial data will soon become a commodity owned and managed by customers and not their financial institution. The government is calling for a customer's transaction history, account balances, credit card usage and mortgage repayments to be made available to competitors via APIs by July 2018.

Like many ideas to emerge in the digital era – where there is a constant struggle between realism and evangelism – open banking has its doubters and believers. Attempts to shake up competition in consumer banking are to be applauded. But the Australian Bankers' Association is right in expressing concerns about customer security and privacy.

Interestingly, in the UK, nine in ten consumers surveyed feel uncomfortable with the idea of third-parties accessing their financial data. Similarly, "lack of trust" was one of the key issues identified by Australia's Productivity Commission in its final report on banking data availability and use, which was released in May.

From my own experience in the financial services sector, I know that it is notoriously difficult to persuade customers to switch banking providers. In the UK, the government has mandated that financial institutions make switching easier. Yet in a 2016 report, the UK's Competition and Markets Authority lamented that "only 3% of personal and 4% of business customers switch to a different bank in any year".

So, is open banking the next big thing in banking? Will it really provide consumers with a digital cure to switching inertia? Or will it be yet another example (like Bitcoin, Google Glass, Apple Watch, etc.) of technology over-promising and underdelivering?

At the end of the day, these questions can only be answered by consumers. We'll have to wait and see what happens when open banking is open for business. Some predict that the digital disruption caused by open banking will lead to the death of retail banking. My guess is that hype will again surpass reality, which is why I am not jumping on the open banking bandwagon just yet.

The global research and advisory firm Gartner has developed a graphic called The Hype Cycle. It has been used by the firm since 1995 to show the common pattern of over-enthusiasm, disillusionment and eventual realism that accompanies each new technology and innovation.

My assessment is that open banking is in the "over-enthusiasm" stage right now. As always, I will adopt a watching brief as there is rarely a need to be first to market with new technology. It will be interesting to see whether Australian financial institutions merely comply with the new regulation or actively embrace and promote the open banking concept.

POSTING DATE | 14 AUGUST 2017

COMPETITIONeverywhere

We humans are inherently competitive beings – it's hardwired into our DNA. Indeed, competition is one of the most basic functions of nature. Darwin called it survival of the fittest via natural selection. All living organisms fight for survival in a constant battle of wit and adaptation.

Our ancestors competed for the limited resources available to satisfy their basic need for food, clothing and shelter. Modern-day Homo sapiens vie for higher order needs like jobs and status. In the game of life, we want to be winners in all pursuits including sport, academia, politics and business.

When it comes to business, competition is the basis of the free market economy. Those firms that cannot capture and maintain a profitable market share fall by the wayside. As tough as it sounds, capitalism is the law of the jungle and it separates winners from losers.

I support the cut and thrust of open market competition. More often than not, it produces the best outcomes for consumers. As in the natural world, grow or die is a constant imperative in the business world. Players on the field must remain flexible and have the ability to respond to changing market conditions.

To be sure, I don't believe in unrestrained competition where one wins at any cost. Governments have a role to play in defining the rules of competition so that it's not survival of the most ruthless or the most deceptive. Beyond that, it's up to each market participant to avoid extinction.

All markets have rules, which is why the term "free market" is an oxymoron. In Australia, the Federal Government is the rule-maker, the referee and the umpire – it regulates markets, ensures a fair playing field and enforces the law. Its job is to improve the functioning of the marketplace.

Competition is central to the operation of markets as it fosters innovation, productivity and growth. Importantly, it stops businesses from being complacent and forces them to think constantly of better ways to satisfy customers. In competitive markets, understanding the needs of customers is crucial.

But many organisations make the mistake of developing products and services without reference to customers. This results in organisations suppling products for which there is no demand. Google Glass is an example of this – it was a solution in search of a problem.

Surprisingly, many organisations make the mistake of putting the product cart before the customer horse. Yet it is only after customer needs are known that an organisation can truly be in a position to develop product solutions. All product development, therefore, must start by answering one basic question: What human need/problem are we trying to solve?

In business, beating the competition requires that you stand out from the crowd. The best way to stand out is to solve meaningful customer problems. By tapping into the direct challenges facing its customers, a business gains competitive advantage over others.

Differentiate or perish has long been a mantra of business. When it comes to banking, there are only two things that a customer experiences – people and technology – and these must work hand-in-hand to provide a point of differentiation.

For many financial institutions, that differentiation is customer centricity. Customer centricity, in turn, is about balancing high tech and high touch. Most customers prefer to use technology (high tech) for routine transactions, like paying bills, but want to speak with a mortgage broker (high touch) when taking out a home loan.

However, some banking "experts" assert that we have entered the era of the digital-only customer. Customers in this segment allegedly want no face-to-face relationship with their bank. Digital-only customers may be on the rise, but I'm far from convinced that they are happy to "purchase" higher value services, like financial advice, without some human interaction.

In a 2015 article titled 'The Return of Corporate Strategy in Banking', Bain & Co had this advice: "Differentiation comes not from baseline steps such as moving activities online but rather by sculpting features that will induce customers to take out a mortgage or invest their wealth with one bank over its competitors".

Personal service is still an important element of consumer banking. A 2016 report by global consulting group Accenture noted that "human interaction remains a vital component of customer satisfaction, even in the digital age". Not all banking services, therefore, are ripe for complete automation. For many, particularly older generations, there is an intrinsic human desire to meet those entrusted with managing their money.

Nowadays, it is a given that financial institutions must provide customers with a multitude of platforms, including mobile, to manage their accounts and transactions. But I challenge those who claim that automation will totally rule banking in future and that it will be a case of "humans need not apply". The robots may be coming, but the new financial order will still require a human touch.

Let the competition begin!

POSTING DATE │ 11 SEPTEMBER 2017

LOANserviceability

How much can I borrow? This is the most common question asked by home buyers and should be answered before you go shopping for your dream home or investment property. Knowing up-front how much you can spend will save you disappointment later.

The maximum size of the loan you can manage is largely determined by what is known in banking parlance as "serviceability". Serviceability is your ability to meet, or service, your home loan repayments. Broadly, it is calculated by deducting your expenses and other commitments from your income and is expressed as follows:

> Gross monthly income
>   - tax
>   - existing commitments
>   - new commitments
>   - living expenses
>   - buffer
>   ―――――――――――――――――
>   **= monthly surplus**
>   (aka Net Income Surplus or NIS)

This basic formula (or variant thereof) is used by lenders to ascertain your borrowing power. But each credit provider will have different rules for how it calculates the various component parts. For example, lenders will adjust income down, load expenses up and add an interest rate buffer based on their individual criteria.

It's important to note that all income is not the same, which is why lenders treat individual elements differently. The exception to this is base salary which – as a steady and predictable source of income – is accepted at face value by credit providers in their loan assessment calculations.

Other income, however, is discounted as it is not guaranteed. A classic example is overtime where banks will accept, say, 80 per cent of overtime. But if overtime is regular and ongoing and an integral part of someone's job (police and nurses), it is typically considered in full for serviceability purposes.

Lenders will also accept non-salary items such as bonuses and commissions as income but not at full value as they are less certain than PAYG income. A reduced portion may be taken into consideration as long as there is a history (say, two years) of receiving such payments.

Rental from investment properties is another acceptable form of income, but is given a "haircut" by most lenders. An arbitrary amount (circa 20 per cent) is trimmed off rental income to allow for costs such as property management, council rates and, of course, periods of vacancy.

As well as revealing your income when applying for a loan, you must also declare all your living expenses including the amount you spend on groceries, utilities and en-tertainment. Living expenses vary from household to household. It follows that a young couple with no children will have fewer expenses than a family of six.

Most Australian lenders use the Household Expenditure Measure (HEM) to calculate the living expenses of mortgage applicants. The HEM is based on 600 items in the ABS Household Expenditure Survey. It includes expenditure on absolute basics (food and clothing) and discretionary basics (alcohol and childcare) but excludes non-basic expenses (overseas holidays).

Your lender will compare the living expenses figure you provide with the relevant HEM calculation of the minimum expenses for a family of your size. The higher of these two figures is then used to determine how much you can afford to borrow and comfortably repay.

Another step in calculating how much you can borrow is to subtract the monthly repayments on any existing debt and the monthly repayments on any new debt. Finally, prudent lenders will increase the interest rate on repayments by circa 2 per cent. This creates an interest rate "buffer" that helps ensure you can still service your loan when rates rise.

Once all the above inputs have been computed, the resulting number is your NIS (Net Income Surplus). This is the surplus income available to you after taxes, living expenses and financial commitments. As noted by the banking regulator APRA, "for most banks, the crux of the lending decision is whether or not the NIS is positive".

This however, as APRA notes, "is a simplification, as clearly banks also take into account qualitative factors including whether the borrower is an established customer or not, any past default history, industry of employment and location of the collateral". Also, your Loan to Value Ratio – the proportion of money you intend to borrow compared to the value of the property – will impact the amount you can borrow.

Finally, always remember that you must be comfortable with the quantum of the debt that you take on. Just because a lender is prepared to offer you a $500,000 mortgage, does not mean that you must accept this level of indebtedness. While you may be able to afford a larger loan, the trade-off will likely be the absence of a social life if you overstretch yourself financially.

Take care not to become a victim of mortgage stress.

POSTING DATE │ 27 SEPTEMBER 2017

SOCIAL CHANGES | 3

Social forces are changing our world and the lives of individuals. We are living longer, marrying later and having fewer children. This is because our values, beliefs and attitudes are constantly evolving and impacting the way we live, work and think. Today, we think differently about many things including health, education, the role of women and financial issues. Changing demographics and social patterns are the focus of this chapter with discussion on population growth, excessive consumerism, household budgets, disappearing manners and encore careers.

DISAPPEARINGmanners

Sometimes I think that I was born in the wrong era. I still open the car door for my wife, even though such chivalry is now unfashionable. I still say "please", "thank you" and "excuse me", even though this etiquette seems to have gone out of style. And I still stand aside and wait for others to exit an elevator before entering, even though this gesture is often not reciprocated.

As a contemporary misfit, I'm able to share my opinions on social media (this blog) without resorting to profanities and abuse. I'm capable of riding in an elevator without the need to make or receive a phone call. And I've been able to climb the corporate ladder through hard work and perseverance – not politics and backstabbing.

At the risk of sounding like an old fogey stuck down memory lane, I've decided not to embrace the new social norms of inconsiderate behaviour. I refuse to disturb others by using my mobile phone while in a movie theatre. I refuse to deliberately and habitually run late for meetings and other appointments. And I refuse to give another driver the finger if they cut me off.

Maybe I didn't get the note about decorum going the way of bell-bottoms and black-and-white TVs, but I still believe in the proverb "manners maketh the man". That certainly used to be the case in sport. Tennis great Bjorn Borg was the epitome of stoicism and a role model for fair play. Then along came his foul-tempered and impulsive opponent John McEnroe.

One of McEnroe's rewards for being tennis' poster boy of bad manners was a lucrative contract with Nike. But it's what happened after that that's the really interesting and perverse part of the story. As noted in a 2007 British newspaper article, there was a price to pay for McEnroe's on-court persona:

> The economy of the tennis circuit began to depend on McEnroe's outbursts – bad behaviour was what people came along to see. So McEnroe began to get away with more and more tantrums. The tantrums were expected – they were the done thing. In the end, McEnroe was trapped – he was now the establishment. His bad manners had become the new good manners.

Rudeness is a contagious behaviour that spreads rapidly. Many personalities, like celebrity chef Gordon Ramsay, have imitated McEnroe's obnoxious style. This mimicry – by high profile individuals who should know better – perpetuates the vicious cycle of incivility. Slowly but irreversibly we find ourselves living in an increasingly impolite society.

Perhaps I should just accept that common courtesy is no longer common practice and cease my hankering for the good old days. My fundamental problem is that I was raised by The Golden Rule – the moral precept that asks us to treat others as we would like others to treat ourselves. What's drilled into you as a child tends to stay with you as an adult.

So it's hard for me to embrace as acceptable the daily assault of selfish behaviour which pervades modern life. In the "ME" society, many have become self-centred and self-absorbed – just look at the obsession with taking selfies. Young people today are significantly more narcissistic than previous generations and have scant time or regard for niceties.

As a society, we no longer mind our Ps and Qs and this is reflected in declining social graces. Coarse language is now part of daily discourse. Contempt for authority is rife. Neighbours treat each other with distrust and suspicion. Town hall meetings have become screaming matches. And aggressive louts make it unsafe to walk the streets at night.

If we had a modicum of respect for basic decency, we would take our hats off during the national anthem. We would cover our mouths when sneezing or coughing. We would stand up when shaking hands with someone. We would revere the elderly and learn from their experiences. And we would wait our turn and not shamelessly queue-jump.

Call me a fuddy-duddy, but I believe that manners are timeless and I hope that they come back in vogue. Parents have a big role to play here. The one thing that I repeatedly drilled into my kids when they were growing up was "never lower your standards". This is indelibly etched in their brains and I am proud of their conduct as adults and now as parents themselves.

Herein endeth my rant. Excuse me if I hath gone on too long. Apologies for any offence caused. Thank you for your attention. Please have a pleasant day.

POSTING DATE | 5 JUNE 2017

WORKPLACEpsychopaths

At some stage in our careers, most of us encounter a horrible boss or colleague. They exist in every sector of the business world and are not as rare as you might think. In many organisations, you will find at least one ruthless individual who will do almost anything to advance their own cause.

In my forty-year career, I have been truly fortunate to have worked with some outstanding individuals. I have also had the misfortune to work for two bosses who I would classify as textbook corporate psychopaths. Both were superficially charming to their superiors and downright rude to their subordinates.

This modus operandi is the classic "psycho-path" to success strategy. Turn on the charisma to those in power and behave with malice towards underlings. Adept at manipulating relationships, the psychopath is able to impress their immediate manager while wreaking havoc on more junior workers.

Such split personality behaviour enables workplace monsters to create successful careers. They exaggerate and lie their way into favour while leaving a wake of destruction in their path. They have no compunction about trampling over others as they lack empathy.

They are so caught up in their own world that it's not in their DNA to consider the feelings and viewpoints of others. The only thing that matters is achieving their self-serving agenda – even if that means sticking the knife into someone standing in their way.

In my personal experience, psychopaths are also control freaks who are not all that intelligent. So they act as bloodsuckers, stealing the ideas of subordinates and offering them up as their own. Taking credit for the good work of others helps fuel their advancement.

Paradoxically, beneath their bluster, psychopaths are typically very insecure individuals. They often feel intellectually threatened by their subordinates (so they hijack ideas) and are adroit at quickly shifting the blame for anything that goes wrong.

Of course, it's difficult to sack a subordinate who is very good at their job. Even a psychopathic boss is smart enough to know that you can't remove a high achiever by claiming poor performance. So the boss resorts to character assassinations, half-truths and innuendos to undermine the employee.

Corporate psychopaths are masters at playing people off against each other. They will tell one story to one person and a different version of the same story to another. This behaviour is designed to manipulate the perception of colleagues against the employee being targeted by the boss.

The target ultimately becomes the victim of a cunning web of deceit. The boss stands victorious while the target is vanquished. The wrong person comes out on top and this was the subject of a *Harvard Business Review* article, 'Why bad guys win at work'. To quote from the article, psychopathic tendencies:

facilitate both the seduction and intimidation tactics that frighten potential competitors and captivate bosses. This explains why individuals with these personality characteristics are often great actors, as well as succeeding in (short-term) sexual relationships. Yet it is important to understand that all these individual gains come at the expense of the group.

British academic Clive Boddy blames the psychopathic behaviour of business leaders for the Global Financial Crisis (GFC). In an article he wrote for the UK *Journal of Business Ethics*, he argued that such people "largely caused the crisis" because their "single-minded pursuit of their own self-enrichment and self-aggrandisement to the exclusion of all other considerations has led to an abandonment of the old-fashioned concept of noblesse oblige, equality, fairness, or of any real notion of corporate social responsibility".

In his paper examining the behaviours which gave rise to the GFC, Boddy had the following to say about corporate psychopaths:

> They seem to be unaffected by the corporate collapses they have created. They present themselves as glibly unbothered by the chaos around them, unconcerned about those who have lost their jobs, savings, and investments, and as lacking any regrets about what they have done. They cheerfully lie about their involvement in events, are very persuasive in blaming others for what has happened and have

no doubts about their own continued worth and value. They are happy to walk away from the economic disaster that they have managed to bring about, with huge payoffs and with new roles advising governments how to prevent such economic disasters.

In a blog post that I published in September last year titled *Conduct risk*, I opined that "the GFC was brought about by having the wrong people wedded to the wrong philosophy". In an earlier post that I published in May 2009 I wrote that "banking is an industry built on trust and the challenge facing regulators and boards is to devise a way of identifying and weeding out megalomaniacs with delusions of global domination".

Of course, this is easier said than done. According to research, up to one in five bosses could be psychopaths. Believe it or not, the same research suggests that psychopaths are as prevalent in the corporate sector as they are in prisons.

At the end of the day, organisations have their share of psychopaths. This condition is not a mental illness but a personality disorder. Regrettably, that distinction does not help employees whose boss' behaviour makes them quake in their boots. Yep, life is not always fair.

POSTING DATE | 28 NOVEMBER 2016

WHISTLEBLOWERbacklash

> *The only thing necessary for the triumph*
> *of evil is for good men to do nothing*
> Edmund Burke

Edmund Burke was an 18th century Irish philosopher, orator and political theorist. His much-quoted triumph-of-evil statement and his interventionist notion of good require us to speak up against wrongdoings. Evil prevails when we turn a blind eye to something that is not right.

But we often remain silent in the face of wrongs and for good reason – fear of reprisal. Dissidents who report misconduct typically face negative repercussions. Consequences can include the loss of one's job for a corporate whistleblower, to physical assault for a Good Samaritan coming to the aid of another.

While good people should be lauded, they can become victims themselves. Retaliation is often heavy-handed and represents a second form of misconduct. Little wonder, then, that observers and bystanders choose not to intervene lest they come under attack for challenging the status quo.

Transgression occurs in all social settings. Examples include domestic violence in homes, sexual abuse in institutions, cyber-bullying in schools, employee harassment in workplaces and initiation rituals in military barracks. These all cross the line in terms of acceptable behaviour.

Of course, wrongdoings are not confined to physical mistreatment. Unacceptable behaviour also includes illegal practices like white-collar crime and harmful activities of corporations which endanger the safety of workers, consumers and the environment.

Whistleblowers often find themselves challenging powerful individuals and institutions. Those in authority work to silence dissenting voices via a range of classic strategies. Truth-tellers are subjected to isolation, humiliation and vilification, with many suffering emotionally and financially.

[Please allow me to insert a parenthetical note here. What is happening right now in America in terms of abuse of power is scandalous. President Trump strong-arms anyone who stands in his way. His impulsive attacks on judges, journalists and officials are unprecedented and threaten the rule of law. Yet the president's own party is protecting him as he lurches from crisis to crisis.

Beyond the press and judiciary, the third check on a president's power is meant to be Congress. This is the branch of government that the Founding Fathers envisioned as the main check and balance on presidential authority. Regrettably, the Republican-controlled Congress is behaving like a lapdog and has put up few roadblocks to Trump's displays of dominance.

In the words of Edward Luce, Washington columnist and commentator for the *Financial Times:* "America's government is at a dangerous impasse. Most people know Mr. Trump is unfit to be commander-in-chief. But nobody with the power to redress it has found the courage to act".]

Those who make public interest disclosures often do so at a high personal cost. The backlash can be severe and dogged determination is required to expose illegal or objectionable practices. A whistleblower's life is never quite the same after the fateful decision to speak out.

Many who publicly "name and shame" feel let down by official channels and regret coming forward. They quickly discover that the organisation or institution concerned would prefer to keep the truth hidden. Alleged perpetrators are often protected with no action taken to stop or remedy the reported wrongdoing.

When it comes to organisational life, the wrongdoing does not even have to be illegal or a breach of policy. Sometimes it can be a case of seriously poor judgment which needs to be called out to protect an organisation from reputational harm and I have had first-hand experience of that scenario.

Many years ago, I found myself in a situation where – along with other colleagues – I wanted to raise concerns about something that I could clearly see was going to severely hurt the organisation. That something was a pet project of the CEO, but he was not receptive to negative feedback.

During a meeting I attended with the CEO about the project, one of my colleagues tactfully and politely informed him that our customers were unlikely to support his pet project (a new product). The CEO exploded, publicly berating and absolutely humiliating my colleague.

The CEO's behaviour sent a clear and powerful message that he was not to be challenged. He created strong social cues and exerted overt pressure on the management team to "get on board" or suffer the consequences. We were on egg shells as we watched a slow-motion train wreck unfold.

For my part, I had no doubt that the project was going to derail. Given this, I felt a strong moral obligation to do something or risk being derelict in my duties and guilty of wilful blindness. So I sent a polite and diplomatic note to the CEO explaining why our customers were out of step with his thinking.

The reward for my honesty was redeployment to a new but temporary role within the organisation after which I received "voluntary" redundancy. Some months later, the CEO was shown the door by the chairman. His pet project resulted in the company writing off more than $22 million.

No one needs to tell me that doing the right thing can come at a heavy personal cost. Yet I have absolutely no regrets at my decision to try and right a wrong. Ironically, it set me on a path that ultimately led me here to Gateway – and I love being the CEO of this wonderful institution.

While it's proverbially said that "no good deed goes unpunished," in my case the end result was worth the pain. However, never underestimate the perils of speaking out. It's certainly not for the fainthearted and it's fraught with danger. I hope that I never have to do it again – but I would, as my moral compass would compel me to do so.

POSTING DATE │ 29 MAY 2017

EXPERTopinions

It seems that the world is full of talking heads masquerading as experts. These pretenders pop up following every breaking news story – from major incidences like terrorist attacks to routine events like interest rate hikes. The media feels compelled to call upon these "authorities" to act as instant experts and explain what has happened and why.

But these so-called pundits are often no more than self-proclaimed gurus. Indeed, they typically know little more than the rest of us. But put them in front of a microphone and these publicity seekers can't resist asserting their opinions on subjects about which they have little or no formal training or expertise.

The Y2K computer bug is a classic example. While technology legend Bill Gates saw the millennium bug as a "minor inconvenience", less qualified IT commentators promulgated doomsday scenarios and were aided in their deception by the media who spun compelling but inaccurate stories.

A gullible public bought into the outrageous predictions about planes falling from the sky and missiles self-launching. But the bug did not bite and the New Year passed with nothing more than the expected hangover. Those who foretold of a global computer apocalypse caused unnecessary panic but were never brought to account.

Nothing had changed by the time of the Fukushima power plant disaster in 2011. Yet again, the media wheeled out instant experts who hyperventilated over the very modest amounts of radioactive fallout. Fears about radiation contamination were clearly overblown but made for dramatic headlines which trumpeted the dangers of nuclear energy.

A report released five years after the disaster by the United Nations Scientific Committee on the Effects of Atomic Radiation (UNSCEAR) found that not one person had died because of the meltdown. Referencing the UNSCEAR report, a *Forbes* magazine article stated:

> No one will die from Fukushima radiation, there will be no increased cancer rates, the food supply is not contaminated, the ocean nearby is not contaminated, most of the people can move back into their homes, and most of the other nuclear plants in Japan can start up just fine.

Almost three years to the day after Fukushima, the world was gripped by the mysterious disappearance of a Malaysian Airlines Boeing 777. The aircraft vanished without a trace, bringing a raft of know-it-alls out of the woodwork. They went into overdrive speculating about what may have happened to the plane.

Many of their theories were not supported by a shred of solid evidence. Nonetheless, their views were given air time by media outlets. This helped networks maintain rolling coverage of the tragedy and filled the huge gap in reliable information about the plane's fate.

Suggestions from armchair sleuths, aviation experts and conspiracy theorists were broadcast. Fringe theories flourished and ranged from the sinister (electronic warfare), to the far-fetched (remote island landing), to the insane (abducted by aliens).

The above examples prove that it's relatively easy for someone to claim to be an expert, but experts (real or imagined) get it wrong all the time. In his book, *Future Babble: Why Expert Predictions Fail - and Why We Believe Them Anyway,* investigative journalist Dan Gardner reveals the repeated and sometimes monumental failure of expert predictions in every field.

Gardner reveals that he's "always been fascinated in the way that experts are held up as gurus and taken so terribly seriously and when their predictions fail, people just shrug and walk away". He argues that the average pundit is about as reliable as flipping a coin.

To support this view, Gardner draws on the work of Philip Tetlock, a professor of psychology at the University of California at Berkeley. Following extensive research, Tetlock discovered that experts' predictions were no more precise than random guesses. Tetlock concluded that "experts are about as accurate as dart-throwing monkeys".

History is littered with examples of seers who got it wrong. Yet, as Gardner notes, the general public continues to put great faith in experts who never lose their widespread appeal. I'm with Gardner when he says that "the future will forever be shrouded in darkness".

Expert predictions fail because the world is complicated, yet our flawed quest for certainty continues. Only fools or geniuses try to predict the future – and I'm neither!

POSTING DATE | 7 AUGUST 2017

HERDmentality

Playing follow the leader is fun as a child, but blindly following others as an adult can be disastrous. Nonetheless, it occurs every day in all walks of life. Being part of the crowd is much safer than going out on a limb. So we tend to conform to conventional wisdom as there's strength in numbers.

Moving in lockstep with peers was one of the causes of the Global Financial Crisis. Bank after bank after bank slavishly ran with the mob down the subprime loan path. Investing in poor-quality loans became fashionable based on the flawed logic that "everyone is doing it and everyone can't be wrong".

Borrowers also displayed "irrational exuberance" with many American households joining the stampeding herd on a speculative frenzy to buy an overpriced property. What was supposed to be a safe bet turned out to be a financial calamity for millions of homeowners when the housing bubble burst.

Taking cues from others occurs in all areas of business. Indeed, it's easy to see what's in vogue in the corporate world. You need only look at the high-priced conferences and conventions for each industry sector to gauge the prevailing trends and hot topics.

Keynote speakers and other "experts" share their wisdom with the assembled throng. Impressionable delegates readily embrace ideas that sound right or appealing without subjecting them to serious challenge or scrutiny. It's easier to go with the flow than to make independent judgments.

But persuasive podium speakers do not have crystal balls. They are not modern-day soothsayers and typically know little more than the rest of us. Yet many followers succumb to the hype of these "thought leaders", lest they be isolated from the mainstream – but not me.

For years, I have refused to jump on the "cash is going to disappear soon" bandwagon. Even though I have been beckoned by the herd to get on board, a sober assessment shows that cash remains a major method of payment and store of value throughout the world.

In the US, the value of currency in circulation is at its highest level, relative to GDP, since the 1950s. In Australia, the value of banknotes in circulation as a share of GDP is at a 50-year high. Over recent years, the ratio of cash to GDP has also grown in Japan and the Eurozone. Despite expert predictions to the contrary, we won't be saying goodbye to cash any time soon.

Nor will human workers be consigned to history. Yet the speaker circuit is replete with scaremongers warning that we will all be replaced by robot workers. People are being tricked into fearing artificial intelligence (AI) to the point where some in the human herd fear extinction from robots that turn rogue.

I challenge this mortal danger scenario and am happy to throw a big bucket of cold water on the sensational claim that robots are going to take over the world. I will undoubtedly be shunned by some in the tech-herd for not falling into line, but I refuse to be hoodwinked by robotic nonsense and I am not alone.

Michael Littman is a professor of computer science at Brown University. He readily acknowledges that every new technology brings its own nightmare scenarios and that AI and robotics are no exceptions. In an opinion editorial, 'Rise of the Machines is Not a Likely Future', he states:

> Let's get one thing straight: A world in which humans are enslaved or destroyed by superintelligent machines of our own creation is purely science fiction. Like every other technology, AI has risks and benefits, but we cannot let fear dominate the conversation or guide AI research.

Professor Littman views dread predictions of computers suddenly waking up and turning on us as unrealistic. He concludes his editorial by imploring that we "please keep the discussion (about AI) firmly within the realm of reason and leave the robot uprisings to Hollywood screenwriters".

I congratulate Professor Littman for his rational assessment and for being a voice of reason in a crowd that seems hell-bent on promulgating a pending AI apocalypse. That crowd includes Silicon Valley and tech-CEOs whose perceived expertise draws others into their "me-too" groupthink.

The world would be a better place with more independent and informed thinkers – particularly when it comes to politics. The frightening rise of populism in politics is another example of herd mentality. Herds are easily influenced by political leaders and demagogues and this has driven angry populist uprisings.

The current day peddlers of populism are appealing to the prejudices of crowds by tapping into prevailing anti-immigration and anti-trade sentiments. But the populist framing of problems invariably leads to the wrong policy responses such as the desire to build walls and erect trade barriers.

When all is said and done, humans will always be herd animals. It's part of our DNA and a throwback to our ancestors' need to band together to survive in the wild. But we can choose not to automatically run with the pack, when necessary. It's challenging, but it can be done.

Take it from one who knows – it's far more interesting being the sheepdog than the sheep.

POSTING DATE │ 19 FEBRUARY 2018

POPULATIONclock

Sometimes my mind wanders and I find myself pondering the most unusual things. It happened again recently when, out of the blue, a thought popped into my head about global population. I suddenly found myself sub-consciously asking: How many humans have ever been born?

Finding the answer to this intriguing question saw me consult several websites. I was going around in circles until I hit upon the work of the Washington-based Population Reference Bureau (PRB). The PRB is a private, non-profit organisation that studies population-related issues.

The PRB collects, analyses and disseminates demo-graphic data. Its most popular article ever, *'How Many People Have Ever Lived on Earth?'*, was first published in 1995. It was subsequently updated in 2002 and 2011. I managed to locate further PRB statistics up to 2015.

Demographic researchers at the PRB estimate that, as of 2015, 108.2 billion people have existed since the dawn of modern humans. By subtracting the 7.4 billion of us who are alive today, we arrive at the figure of 100.8 billion people who have died before us.

From the above data, we can calculate that just under seven per cent of all those ever born were alive in 2015. Viewed from a different perspective, we can say that the dead outnumber the living by almost 14 to 1. This dispels the myth that there are more people alive today than have ever lived.

By delving back into the mists of time, the PRB researchers believe that the first two Homo sapiens (some call them Adam and Eve) walked the Earth about 50,000 BC. At the dawn of agriculture, about 8,000 BC, the population of the world was approximately five million. By AD 1, human population had risen to circa 300 million.

By 1650, the world's population had climbed to about 500 million and then passed the 1 billion mark by 1800. From 1850 until now, the planet's living population has increased by more than sixfold. Last August, the PRB forecast that the Earth will be home to 9.8 billion people by 2050 – an increase of 31 per cent in just 33 years.

The world's population is predicted to hit the 10 billion mark in 2053 if the PRB's 2050 assumptions are applied to subsequent years – and this will impact the dead-to-living ratio. By 2053, the living will make up close to nine per cent of those who have ever been born while the dead will outnumber the living by almost 10 to 1.

Some demographers believe that the world's population will stabilise at 10 billion inhabitants. At that rate of population growth, the living will never outnumber the dead. The number of people alive will always be dwarfed by the number of history's dead.

Throughout most of human history, life expectancy has been very short. Infant mortality in the early days of our existence was very high – perhaps 500 infant deaths per 1,000 births. And in the Middle Ages, many people never made it out of childhood, living only 10–12 years.

Infectious diseases have been the most common cause of death throughout human history by a wide margin. Plagues like the Black Death killed 50 million Europeans in the 14th century – about 60 per cent of Europe's entire population. In contrast, there were 42 million deaths because of World War II in Europe.

We are forever dying, and this impacts contemporary society in myriad ways. For example, Facebook has over one billion users and 30 million of these died in the first eight years of its existence. At the current rate that Facebook users are kicking the bucket – more than 10,000 per day – it is estimated that by 2065 Facebook will have more accounts belonging to the dead than the living.

Not surprisingly, digital condolences are on the rise. Family and friends set up memorial pages for loved ones on social media sites and this extends the digital footprint of the deceased beyond the grave. Twitter has also become a popular medium to express grief and pay tribute.

Believe it or not, there is even talk of the possibility of offering individuals social media immortality after their biological death. A team of academics from the University of Melbourne put together a brief article explaining how digital afterlife technology (which is in its infancy) allows social media information to be harvested in order to construct a digital personification of the deceased.

As creepy as it sounds, this technology creates an interactive digital avatar of the deceased which can "chat" to other people in the deceased's communication style long after the person has passed away. The avatar is akin to a digital alter-ego, providing some quasi-permanence to a person's existence.

If the futurists are to be believed, the dying will increasingly prefer to be remembered with a virtual space on the Internet rather than a traditional headstone in a cemetery. Personally, I have no desire to blur the line between life and death.

Good grief! When my time is up, I would rather rest in peace than live in cyber-space.

POSTING DATE │ 5 MARCH 2018

JOURNALISTICstandards

Sometimes I feel that I've lost the plot. Increasingly, I find myself at odds with where society is going. For example, I rarely watch the programs they serve up on commercial television. Much of what is on "the box" is mind-numbing and/or unnecessarily sensational and I don't find it entertaining. I'm starting to wonder if I'm from another time.

Current affairs programs used to be no nonsense with broadcast journalists and reporters fearlessly tackling the serious issues of the day. Nowadays, these programs and their "news" presenters offer trivial stories about weight loss, toddler tantrums and back cures. No wonder Gerald Stone observed in his book, *Who Killed Channel 9?: The death of Kerry Packer's mighty TV dream machine*, that commercial TV is pitching to the lowest common denominator.

Commenting on the "dumbing down" of the Channel 9 program *A Current Affair*, Stone wrote:

> Here was a program that once prided itself on a nightly menu filled with hard-hitting interviews, sensational crime investigations and the inside dope on the latest titillating celebrity scandal. More and more it had begun to dwell on diet fads and shopping tips, topped up with melodramatic ambushes of small-time con men, or the inevitable tear-jerkers about battling families who can't pay the rent.

In fairness, I must acknowledge the media's claim that they simply produce what consumers want. As a society, we would rather read about the sordid private lives of celebrities than have a serious debate about the long-term benefits of public policy. So, just as we get the politicians we deserve, we also get the media we deserve.

As citizens, we are complicit with falling standards and they have certainly plummeted. It still staggers me that the reality TV show *Big Brother* was a ratings winner, even though it demeaned contestants, promoted bullying and encouraged sexual behaviour and nudity. *Big Brother* was vulgar and the antics of its participants eroded the distinction between public and private.

Regrettably, standards of taste and decency remain in decline as the quality of television programs continues to deteriorate. We seem to have become conditioned to a diet of explicit sex, coarse language and graphic violence with such content now considered the norm. Tabloid television has modelled itself on its close kin, the tabloid press.

Tabloid journalists – the tawdry cousins of broadcast journalists – are known for sensationalism in reporting. Sex, scandals and beat-ups are the order of the day. Journalists must fill column space for their editors by "finding" stories. Many operate under the mantra "Never let the truth get in the way of a good story" in order to whip readers into a frenzy.

There are, of course, many fine and ethical journalists who work outside of the irreverent tabloid world. These individuals fulfil a vital role in society. A true democracy requires the active participation of an informed public, which is only possible if citizens have unfettered access to information. Ironically, the phone hacking scandal in Britain only came to public attention due to the free press.

In response to the scandal, *The Telegraph* in London published the following editorial.

> This newspaper cares passionately about maintaining the highest standards of journalism. We believe that journalism, when practised properly, protects the public from abuses of power by exposing those who are guilty of dishonesty, corruption or injustice. Journalism that harms the innocent – by telling lies or spreading falsehoods about them, or by unjustifiably invading their privacy – does the exact opposite of what good journalism aims to achieve.

Hear, hear! Unfortunately, not all journalists and/or media outlets ascribe to this level of professionalism. And that's not just my opinion – many mainstream journalists also lament falling standards of truthfulness, accuracy, objectivity, impartiality and fairness. One senior Australian journalist put it this way:

> I've spent my working life as a journalist ... But now, reading the newspapers and watching the news, I can't help but wonder if this is a craft that is not only losing its centre of corporate gravity and support, but also some fundamental sense of its mission and responsibility ... the major market tabloids ... are the dominant organs of news in all our capital cities. They cry wolf, they cry terror, they fan the flames of disquiet and distrust. Because fear sells.

In his 2011 book, *Sideshow: dumbing down democracy*, former federal government minister Lindsay Tanner was withering in his critique of the media. He cited several examples where the media created unnecessary panic including the Global Financial Crisis, the Year 2K computer bug and the swine flu epidemic. The media reporting of these events produced a public response out of proportion to the threat.

The power of the media comes from its ability to influence and shape the perception of the public. We look to the media to tell us what is happening in the world as we don't have the time or skills to sift through vast amounts of information ourselves. The media sets the news agenda and political tone and this informs our decision-making as citizens.

The free press plays a vital role in society and can serve citizens by exposing wrongdoings and informing debates. However, it is disappointing to note that some sections of the media do not operate to the highest ethical standards. No wonder that in Australia – and other parts of the world – journalists are among the least trusted professionals.

POSTING DATE │ 23 MAY 2016

EXCESSIVEconsumerism

Around the world, more and more people are focussed on projecting the right image and social status. From the car we drive, to the clothes we wear and the suburb we live in, conspicuous consumption – once the sole preserve of the rich and famous – has come to the masses.

Many households live by the mantra: "We want it, we want it now and we're not prepared to wait". But the more we have, the more we want, and this is fuelling an endless cycle of spending. We increasingly define our lives by how much stuff we have and many find it difficult to control the urge to splurge.

Adopting a materialistic lifestyle invariably leads to comparisons with others. We covet thy neighbour's trophy home, we are jealous of our friend's fancy car and we envy our colleague's luxury holiday. Our happiness is diminished if we believe that the grass is greener on the other side.

For many, wellbeing is determined more by relative wealth than absolute wealth. At its worst, keeping up with the Joneses can become an obsession, causing us to rack up debt on showy material goods. We delight in revealing to the world that we've made it and then brag about it on social media.

Paradoxically, while we see others as "The Joneses", they often see us as the ones to emulate and they, in turn, try to outdo us. So a vicious cycle of one-upman-ship begins. Always restless, constantly wanting more and never content with what we have, the race to get ahead continues apace.

As a nation, we suffer from "affluenza". Australian households are the most heavily indebted in the world, owing a record $2 trillion to banks and other lenders. Global comparisons of personal debt typically look at the total owed versus a country's gross domestic product (GDP).

In the first quarter of 2016, the Bank for International Settlements reported that Australia had a ratio of 125 per cent personal debt to GDP. This is an all-time high and has given Australia the dubious honour of being the country with the highest household debt to GDP ratio.

Whether this level of household debt is sustainable is hotly debated. Most is "good debt" (used to buy homes), but that should not make us complacent. The sobering reality is that, by international standards, we shoulder the biggest debts relative to our incomes.

Australia's household debt is almost four times higher than our nation's public debt, which sits at 34 per cent of GDP. This is one of the lowest government debt levels in the OECD. Ironically, there are constant cries to reduce this negligible level of sovereign debt while the real culprit – household debt – goes unchecked.

Last October, the International Monetary Fund (IMF) warned that Australian households are on a potentially dangerous debt binge. In its *Fiscal Monitor* report, the IMF singled out Australia as one of the few countries where private debt is increasing and bucking the global trend.

Our world-beating private debt was also the subject of a 2016 report by LF Economics. Their report, *Australia's*

Addiction to Debt, claims that "the exponential surge in mortgage debt issuance over the last two decades has generated the largest housing bubble in Australian economic history".

Of course, not every Australian household has a super-sized mortgage and not every individual is an aspirational spender. But those living a minimalist life are certainly in the minority. The mass media tells us we deserve the best and that it's our right to go for it – and the majority of us do!

At the end of the day, it's up to each of us to live the life we want. We are all wired to seek pleasure. But happiness and fulfillment mean different things to different people. When it comes to money, the important point to note is that buying things cannot make you happy beyond a superficial level.

Please allow me to conclude with a question. In both my professional and personal life, I have observed that the overwhelming majority of people believe that if they had just a little more money, they would be happier. The question for all of us is this: At what stage does that little bit more become enough?

POSTING DATE | 13 MARCH 2017

NUMBERsystems

No one knows with absolute certainty when humans started counting. Some archaeological evidence suggests that the genesis of numbers and counting may go back 30,000 years. What we do know is that a formal system of numbers was developed by the Sumerian and Babylonian civilisations of Mesopotamia (roughly, modern Iraq) and in ancient Egypt.

Numbers are an integral part of our everyday lives. We use maths without even thinking about it. From figuring out the amount needed to buy a coffee, to calculating the interest earned on a bank deposit, we are surrounded by numbers. We use numbers to tell the time, measure height, analyse trends, set budgets, quantify risk, rank athletes and forecast outcomes.

Numbers have enabled humanity to solve countless problems. Mathematics has helped us understand the cycles of nature and unlock some of the mysteries of the universe. Humanity's rapid progress over the past century in commerce, science and technology has been driven by mathematics. Nowadays, it's a case of business by numbers.

Dome-headed mathematicians used to become school teachers. Today, number-crunchers are in strong demand in business, with some deployed to write computer algorithms. Algorithms are behind Google's search results and Amazon's book recommendations. Not surprisingly, Google's founders, Sergey Brin and Larry Page, are both mathematicians.*

---

* The word "Google" is a misspelling of the mathematical term "googol", which means a number represented by 1 followed by 100 zeros.

In tracing the very first number system, we find the most ancient evidence of counting in notches carved into lengths of bone. From this simple tallying method, humans progressed to rudimentary arithmetic and then, thanks to the Sumerian people in 3100 BC, to a sexagesimal (base 60) numeral system which was transmitted to the Babylonians.

The sexagesimal system is still used today to measure angles (360 degrees in a circle), determine time (60 seconds in a minute, 60 minutes in an hour) and calculate geographic coordinates (360° of longitude and 180° of latitude). Both the sphere of a globe and the circular face of a clock owe their divisions to the Babylonians.

The next milestone in mathematics occurred around 2700 BC with the development by the ancient Egyptians of a decimal system. This system used seven different symbols (hieroglyphics) with each symbol representing a power of 10, viz. one, ten, one hundred, one thousand, ten thousand, one hundred thousand and one million.

From as early as 2500 BC, the Egyptians were writing fractions and used their acquired mathematical literacy largely for engineering purposes. They also created a system of algebra and geometry, enabling them to build the great pyramids and other breathtaking monuments, such as the Sphinx, with extreme accuracy.

The mathematical techniques of the Egyptians were passed on to the ancient Greeks. The Greeks quickly built upon this knowledge and made important contributions of their own. For example, the great mathematician

Pythagoras (c.570–c.495 BC) developed his theorem of right-angled triangles. He was also the first person to come up with the idea of odd and even numbers.

The Pythagorean theorem is especially important today to construction workers and architects. It allows them to ascertain the proper dimensions for building structures and bridges which are safe and stable. The theorem is most commonly applied to triangular-shaped roofs and gables and is also used by builders to lay the foundation for the corners of a building.

By the middle of the 1st century BC, the Romans had tightened their grip on the Greek empire and halted the mathematical revolution of the Greeks. No mathematical innovations occurred under the Roman Empire. Roman numerals were the dominant number system for trade and administration in most of Europe for over a millennium. However, the Roman system was flawed as it had no symbol for zero.

Around 200 BC, the Indians invented the number "zero" and this is still considered India's greatest contribution to the world. They incorporated a zero into their numbering system – which ran from zero to nine. These came to be called Arabic numerals as they spread first to Islamic countries before reaching Europe around AD 1200.

Given this background, it is self-evident why the system of numbers we use today – 0, 1, 2, 3, 4, 5, 6, 7, 8, 9 – is referred to as the Hindu-Arabic numeral system or Indo-Arabic numerals. Unlike earlier numeral systems, these 10 digits can be used in combination to represent all possible numbers. The word "digit" literally means finger or toe.

Humanity has certainly come a long way from adding and subtracting on fingers!

POSTING DATE │ 13 JUNE 2016

SEXsells

Now that I've got your attention, I'd like to tell you the ugly truth about beauty. We humans love to pretend. We claim that looks don't matter, but they do. Studies have shown that attractive people do better in life. This may not be fair or politically correct, but research reveals that it is the case.

Attractive people tend to have better jobs, earn more money and live happier lives. They are typically hired sooner and promoted quicker than less attractive colleagues. Good-looking workers often have greater self-esteem and this is appealing to employers.

There is a payoff to looking good, and noted labour economist Daniel Hamermesh examines the advantages of beauty in his book, *Beauty Pays*: *Why Attractive People Are More Successful*. Professor Hamermesh is the acknowledged father of pulchronomics – the economic study of beauty.

He shows that beauty's rewards are not superficial and reveals that looks have a bigger impact on our lifetime earning power than education. Hamermesh demonstrates how society favours the beautiful and how better-looking people experience undeniable benefits in all aspects of life.

That the genetically blessed get more is not a surprise to most of us. It's easier for beautiful people to find mates. Also, those most pleasing to the eye often enjoy special treatment – like attractive women receiving priority when entering a venue – otherwise called Nightlife Economics 101.

This beauty bias is all around us. Voters prefer better-looking candidates. Students prefer better-looking professors. Teachers prefer better-looking students. And, believe it or not, mothers have been shown to favour their more attractive children.

Having model looks certainly helps when it comes to celebrity endorsements. Anna Kournikova's striking appearance made her one of the best-known tennis stars ever. In her prime, she was the world's most marketable sportswoman even though she never won a major singles title.

What she did win was sponsorship deals worth millions of dollars as her sex appeal transcended tennis. As one tennis journalist observed: "She got a lot more attention and a lot more endorsement money than a lot of players who were better than her".

Human beings naturally gravitate towards beautiful things like a breathtaking waterfall. So it's not surprising that we use our senses to make snap judgments about others based on their looks. Appearance-based stereotypes abound causing us to categorise people as too fat, too thin, too short and so on.

After extensive studies over three decades on physical attractiveness, researcher Dr Gordon Patzer concluded that human beings are hardwired to respond more favourably to attractive people. "Good-looking men and women are generally regarded to be more talented, kind, honest and intelligent than their less attractive counterparts," he noted.

Several scholars see appearance-based discrimination as a civil rights issue for "the unattractive class". In her book, *The Beauty Bias: The Injustice Of Appearance In Life And Law*, Stanford law professor Deborah Rhode argues that this bias infringes fundamental rights, compromises merit principles and reinforces debilitating stereotypes.

Sociologist Catherine Hakim believes there is another way for the less attractive to fight back. In her provocative book, *Honey Money: The Power of Erotic Capital*, she ruffles more than a few feathers by suggesting that women can enhance their power "in the bedroom and the boardroom" by using erotic capital. She describes this as:

> a fluid but crucial combination of liveliness, sex appeal, beauty, social skills and attractive styling – a mixture of physical and social attractiveness which makes someone an agreeable colleague, attractive to everyone they meet, at work or in private.

I don't believe that one's progress in life should be based on survival of the prettiest. Notwithstanding this egalitarian view, I do acknowledge that we live in a world where outer appearance often trumps inner beauty. However, I don't accept that glamorous people (e.g. Marilyn Monroe) are necessarily happier than the rest of us.

Beauty is only skin deep, so let me conclude with more than a ray of hope for the less attractive. Remember the nerds at school? They were the brainy but socially awkward group who suffered daily schoolyard insults. Thanks to the digital revolution, many of these "four-eyed geeks" – like Bill Gates – have achieved unprecedented power and influence.

We should celebrate the fact that geeks are no longer social outcasts. Paradoxically, it is the tech-heads who have inherited the Earth – not the bold and beautiful!

POSTING DATE │ 4 OCTOBER 2016

WORLDfacts

Earlier this year an interesting book landed on my desk. It was sent to me by *The Economist* as a reward for being a subscriber to their weekly print magazine. The book, *Pocket World in Figures: 2016 Edition* is the 25th anniversary edition of this annual tome.

The book provides an intriguing snapshot of the world today on a diverse range of subjects. It gives rankings on everything from crime, to culture and tourism, to transport. It even contains The Big Mac Index which is a light-hearted guide as to whether currencies are at their correct level, based on the theory of parity purchasing power.

With rankings on more than 300 topics, data on over 180 countries and detailed profiles of more than 65 of the world's major economies, *Pocket World* is a treasure trove of fascinating statistics that both inform and entertain. Here is a cross-section of attention-grabbing facts about our world. (Note that all figures are based upon the latest available sources in 2015.)

Men in Sierra Leone have the lowest life expectancy at 46.5 years. Women in Qatar top the scales regarding the percentage (49.7) who are obese. Marriages in Guam are the least likely to last with 4.6 divorces per 1,000 people per year. The citizens of French Polynesia have the world's highest rate of diabetes – 24.4 per cent of the adult population.

Looking at the world through an economic lens is equally interesting. The US boasts the world's biggest economy with GDP of US$16,768 billion. Monaco has the highest GDP per head of population at US$173,377. South Sudan has the lowest economic growth with its economy shrinking by 8.4 per cent of GDP. Venezuela holds the humiliating distinction of having the highest rate of inflation across the globe – a punishing 62.2 per cent.

When it comes to crop commodities, China is the biggest producer of rice with annual output of 142.5 million tonnes. Brazil is the number one coffee grower with its plantations producing 2.9 million tonnes per annum. Meanwhile, the Ivory Coast leads the cultivation of cocoa beans producing 1.75 million tonnes annually.

If you think getting a job in Australia is hard, spare a thought for the citizens of Namibia. That nation wins first prize in the highest rate of unemployment category at an alarming 29.7 per cent. Bosnia and Herzegovina has an even greater problem with youth unemployment reaching a devastating 60.4 per cent. And if you don't like long hours, stay clear of Turkey where the average hours worked per week is 49.

When it comes to education, I'm pleased to report that Australia tops one of the categories – highest secondary school enrolment (as a percentage of the relevant age group). The gong for the world's number one university goes to Harvard. Cuba has the highest level of investment in education – an impressive 12.8 per cent of GDP. Niger has the least literate population with a paltry 15.5 per cent able to read and write.

As we live in a digital world, *Pocket World* includes some interesting statistics on the use of technology.

The citizens of Hong Kong are most likely to buy a new computer with 336.6 machines sold in 2013 per 1,000 people. Iceland has the highest proportion of Internet users with an astonishing 96.6 per cent of the population online. Macau tops the chart for mobile phone ownership with a whopping 304.1 phones for every 100 citizens.

Of course, our world also has a darker side. Honduras has earned the ignominious honour of being the murder capital of the world with the most homicides – 91 per 100,000 pop. Belgium too wears an unenviable crown – that of the nation with the most robberies at 1.7 per 100,000 pop. The US incarcerates its wrongdoers at a rate greater than any other nation – 698 per 100,000 pop.

On a more light-hearted note, the Czech Republic downs the most beer per head – 145.4 litres per year. The Lebanese are the heaviest smokers in the world, puffing an average of 8 cigarettes per day. The people of Iceland are the planet's most avid moviegoers with Icelanders, on average, visiting the flicks 5 times during 2013.

It is with some embarrassment that I reveal that Australia is the gambling capital of the world. Aussies love a punt and we lose more on gambling per person than any other nation – an average of $1,105 in 2014 for every man, woman and child. No wonder popular folklore says that "Australians will bet on two flies crawling up a wall"!

Australians also hold another title – that of the most indebted household sector in the world. Australian households are awash with debt and have more debt (leverage) compared to the size of their economy than any other in the world. *Pocket World* lists us as having the fifth highest household debt in 2013 with Denmark in the number one spot. But we Aussies passed the Danes in household debt to GDP in the third quarter of 2015.

Many believe this is where Australia's real debt and deticit problem lies and not, as I have repeatedly pointed out in previous posts, in the public sector.

POSTING DATE │ 26 APRIL 2016

COUNTER-INTUITIVEthinking

Here's the thing I've long argued: The solutions to our problems are often counter-intuitive. The right course of action can be the exact opposite of what we initially thought. The best answer or explanation can challenge our gut instinct and require us to embrace that which does not come naturally and/or defies our deductive rationality.

This is certainly the case within the realms of science. As Galileo demonstrated centuries ago, the truths about the physical universe are often contradictory. We experience the Earth as flat even though we know it is round. Similarly, we see the Sun "rise" and "set" each day, even though we know it stays in its position at the centre of our solar system.

In business, it takes a brave leader to make truly game-changing decisions that go against conventional wisdom. Henry Ford did just that by doubling the wages of his workers in order to attract and retain the talent he needed. His new class of worker was able to afford the very product his company was producing. This expanded the overall market for the Model T and triggered a consumer revolution that helped create the wealthiest nation on Earth.

It's not just the Industrial Revolution that spawned innovative leaders. Our current Digital Revolution boasts many thinkers who challenged the status quo, including the founders of Google. They made the radical choice to give away their products for free and this has made them fabulously rich. Google does not charge Internet users for using its search engine and other services. Rather, it generates 98 per cent of its massive billions in revenue from selling online advertising space.

Google could not attract advertisers without readers – and it needs lots of them. The more readers it attracts, the more interest that is generated from advertisers. So Google lures in users, collects their data and then sells access to eager advertisers across the planet. The more Google knows about an individual, the better it can target ads and therefore the more it can charge for ad space.

Of course, unconventional solutions are not limited to the business world. Take for example the nursing home that was faced with a serious problem: Some elderly patients with dementia frequently "escaped" from the hospital during episodes of agitation from memory loss. They would walk a block or so, board the first bus that came by and invariably become lost.

Attempts to stop the patients leaving the medical facility resulted in ugly confrontations. So instead of locking the doors to keep patients in, they opened the doors and allowed patients to flee to a fake bus stop built right on the hospital's doorstep. The patient would eventually calm down, accept that no buses were running that day and peacefully return to the hospital.

A more controversial example of upside-down thinking is drug addiction. Treating heroin addicts by giving them heroin might seem incongruous, but trials in Switzerland show that administering heroin in supervised clinics can produce better results than conventional methadone treatments.

If you frame the drug problem as a medical dependency and not a criminal offence, users will be helped by trained nurses rather than arrested by burly police officers. Yes, it does seem absurd to provide addicts with free synthetic drugs, free needles and paid medical professionals, but it does work in reducing dependency.

Life has taught me that many things are counter-intuitive. I know that open trade creates more jobs than it destroys. I know that government debt is a good thing in times of weak economic growth. I know that there's not a direct correlation between hours worked and work performed. And I know that the biggest risk in life is not taking any risks.

Our natural instinct is to play it safe when making decisions and solving problems. But turning long-held beliefs on their head can lead to alternative insights and new thinking. Such breakthrough thinking led to the development of a telephone that isn't just for making calls. Now, where would we be without our smartphones?

POSTING DATE │ 14 NOVEMBER 2016

LUXURYfever

Australians have a rising appetite for the good things in life. More and more of us crave prestige cars, trophy homes, designer clothes, exotic holidays, gourmet dining and exclusive wines. Even people on modest incomes aspire to own a Louis Vuitton handbag or a Mercedes-Benz sports.

Our chic desires have not gone unnoticed with iconic international retail brands flocking to our shores in droves. Luxury stores such as Fendi, Christian Dior, Chanel, Prada, Tiffany & Co, Salvatore Ferragamo, Burberry and Gucci have set up shop in Australia.

Emulating the lifestyles of the rich and famous is not confined to Australia. Top-end goods are in high demand across the globe. In many developed countries, an almost insatiable appetite for high-end merchandise is fuelling a boom in luxury spending.

Branded capitalism is big business and it's growing. The overall luxury industry is closely tracked by consulting group, Bain & Company. In its latest annual report on the market, Bain & Company reveal that worldwide sales of luxury goods in 2016 surpassed €1 trillion in retail sales value.

For much of human history, the biggest problem faced by Homo sapiens has been *scarcity* – not having enough of what was needed. The economic definition of a *need* is something that is required to survive. Our forebears' needs were very basic – food, water, clothing and shelter.

In contemporary society, our basic needs are being met – you have only to look at the growing rate of obesity to confirm that. So our focus now is on higher order wants. A *want*, in economics, is one notch up from needs and is something that people desire to have, rather than must have.

Today we suffer from an over-abundance of goods and the more we have, the more we want. In their 2005 book, *Affluenza: When Too Much Is Never Enough*, Australian economists Clive Hamilton and Richard Denniss pull no punches in claiming that our society is addicted to over-consumption.

> Our houses are bigger than ever, but our families are smaller. Our kids go to the best schools we can afford, but we hardly see them. We've got more money to spend, yet we're further in debt than ever before. What is going on? The Western world is in the grip of a consumption binge that is unique in human history. We aspire to the lifestyles of the rich and famous at the cost of family, friends and personal fulfilment. Rates of stress, depression and obesity are up as we wrestle with the emptiness and endless disappointments of the consumer life.*

That our non-stop quest for newer and shinier stuff has not delivered greater happiness is not a surprise. As I have opined on previous occasions in this blog, life experiences (like a barbeque with friends) give us more lasting pleasure than material things (like designer shoes).

---

* From the publisher's website

Yet, as a nation, we continue to splurge and have traded up to higher levels of quality and taste. Many of us have become manic shoppers hooked on debt. Materialism clearly comes at a high price and keeping up with the Joneses requires some cunning choices to keep up appearances.

Consumers – not just in Australia but around the world – shop selectively for luxury goods. A *Harvard Business Review* article, 'Luxury for the Masses', put it this way:

> Consumers tend to trade up to the premium product in categories that are important to them but trade down – buying a low-cost brand or private label, or even going without – in categories that are less meaningful to them. Consequently, people's buying habits do not invariably correspond to their income level. They may shop at Costco but drive a Mercedes, or they may buy private-label dishwashing liquid but drink Sam Adams beer.

Notwithstanding record spending by Australian households and record debt, we still talk about the "Aussie battler". This, according to Clive Hamilton, is erroneous.

> We love this idea of the battler … But we are not battlers in any sense. You don't battle to live in Australia. The only battle is to get your BMW through the traffic. Deep down we feel uncomfortable with our affluence and feel guilty about it – so we cling to this myth and focus on the things we don't have.

You have only to scan the seventh annual *Global Wealth Report* (2016) to confirm this myth. Australians, according to the report compiled by Credit Suisse, are the second richest people in the world. The "lucky country" posted an average wealth of US$375,600 (A$508,900) for every Australian. We are second only to Switzerland with an average net worth of US$562,000. The global average is just US$52,800 for each person.

In Australia, perhaps it's a case of "I shop, therefore I am".

POSTING DATE │ 31 JULY 2017

ENCOREcareers

Later this week I will celebrate my 60th birthday and I truly believe that the best is yet to come. The older I get, the happier I become, so turning the big 6-0 is a welcome milestone. I will take entering a new decade in my stride and will forge new and different boundaries.

While I'm already comfortable and content with my lot in life, I'm told that my golden years era, which begins this Friday, will bring new joys. This mature life stage, according to the experts, allows people to do the things that they have always dreamed of.

Apparently, now is the time for people of my vintage to make a bucket list. Unsurprisingly, what tops most lists is overseas travel and chasing once-in-a-lifetime adventures like exploring the Galapagos Islands, witnessing the Northern Lights, driving Route 66 or gambling in Las Vegas.

I'm very fortunate to have already visited some of the globe's most exciting destinations. So my focus – when I eventually retire from full-time work – will be on other things like family and giving back. I believe that reaching 60 is not a finish line but an opportunity for new beginnings.

I find it hard to envisage that I will ever wind down. For me, life has always been about experiences not things. When I ultimately have more time on my hands, I intend to fill that void with an "encore career" – i.e. undertaking paid or volunteer work that has social impact and which fits around my life and not vice versa.

A desire to contribute to the greater good has seen many baby boomers adopt encore careers. Microsoft founder Bill Gates has embraced philanthropic activities, while former US Vice President Al Gore has become an environmental activist.

Few baby boomers want to retire in the traditional sense, i.e., stop everything and just sit at home waiting for death. Rather, they want to reinvent themselves by launching a second "career". In my case, I hope to continue at a more leisurely pace as a mentor, coach or director.

Meantime, my wife and I are putting together a bucket list for when I no longer need to show up every day at the office. Neither Beverley nor I have designs on being aging hipsters zooming around in an open-top red sports car. Rather, our desires are far more pragmatic and include additional time with our seven grandchildren.

Beyond that, my one unfulfilled ambition is to finish writing a book that I started prior to joining Gateway. I am halfway through and it has really bugged me for the past decade that I have not been able to finish it – because they work me too hard here at Gateway!

Being a baby boomer makes me part of one of the largest and most influential age groups in Australia. According to the Australian Bureau of Statistics, there are almost 5.6 million boomers in Australia (those born between 1946 and 1966) with the overwhelming majority now aged in their 50s and 60s.

The baby boomer generation has dominated life around the world for over a half-century and their influence is set to continue. Boomers will impact the workforce as they retire, the housing market as they downsize, the health care system as they age and the welfare system as they run out of money.

The age pension is Australia's single biggest welfare payment. It cost $44 billion in 2015–16 and will grow to $50 billion by 2018–19 or about 10 per cent of total federal budget spending. Clearly, the ripple effect of the aging of the rock 'n' roll generation will also be felt economically.

Regular readers of this blog will know my often-repeated concern that policymakers have yet to grasp the magnitude of the grey demographic tsunami that is sweeping the planet. It is a megatrend that will transform economies and societies in both developed and developing nations.

The world is adding wrinkles and societies will need to adjust accordingly. As for me, I promise that I won't have a "holy sh*t" moment this Friday on becoming a sexagenarian. Sooner or later, Father Time catches up with everyone. I'm confident that I'll cope with another birthday ending in zero.

POSTING DATE | 3 JULY 2017

TRUEcontentment

It's the biggest question we all face and it crops up in everyone's life from time to time. It seems to take on even greater importance as we get older. It's a question that just won't go away. Since the dawn of time, humans have asked: Why are we here?

We all search for a sense of purpose and meaning in our lives. Some of us find it early, while others struggle to understand what it's all about. The path to happiness is different for every person – there's no one roadmap for the journey we each must take.

As we progress through life, it's important to find joy in the journey. In the words of poet Ralph Waldo Emerson, "Life is a journey, not a destination". We never actually "arrive", which is why we need to savour and learn from all of life's experiences – be they hardships and challenges or joy and happiness.

While it's a cliché to say that money does not buy happiness, it's absolutely true. The single-minded pursuit of wealth and possessions puts us on a hedonic treadmill. The more we have, the more we want. We crave the latest and best possessions so that we can keep up with the Joneses.

Ironically, much of our unhappiness in life is the result of comparisons we make with others. We often believe the grass is greener on the other side. We covet thy neighbour's flat screen TV and luxury car, lest we fall behind in the game of life which – for an increasing number of people – is acquiring wealth.

The paradox is that as a society we are becoming richer, not happier. This is revealed in the *World Happiness Report*, which confirms that income alone does not deliver contentment. The happiest countries are those that focus not just on economic outcomes but also on social and environmental development.

The report's co-editor, Professor Jeffrey Sachs from Columbia University, singled out the US as a country that has focussed more on economic growth at the expense of happiness. "There is a very strong message for my country, the United States, which is very rich, has gotten a lot richer over the last 50 years, but has gotten no happier," he said.

So, if having more and more possessions does not make us happier, should we adopt a minimalist approach to life? There is a growing minimalist movement which advocates that we should get by with less. The basic premise of the movement is to live without excessive possessions in order to have more meaningful and thoughtful experiences.

Working against a simpler life are marketers who sow seeds of discontent by bombarding us daily with promotions about products and gadgets that are newer and better. This has created a disorder called compulsive shopping and it afflicts people who get hooked on the adrenalin rush and feeling of euphoria that comes from buying something new – "I shop, therefore I am".

Many of us buy things we don't really need and this particularly applies to clothing. Open your wardrobe and take stock of all the clothes you have either never worn or not worn in the past 12 months. It is claimed that most people wear 20 per cent of their clothes 80 per cent of the time. Put another way, we barely wear 80 per cent of what's in our closet.

As I have opined in this blog on many occasions, life experiences (like a family holiday) give us more lasting pleasure than material possessions (like designer shoes). Yet people often deny themselves experiences (like the joy of giving) in favour of spoiling themselves with material goods.

Shortly after I started my banking career over 40 years ago, I came across some words of wisdom. They were printed on the bottom of the day/date calendar which sat on my desk. While the example used in that 1970s quote is now dated, the message nonetheless remains clear.

> If you want to see what your priorities are in life, just review your cheque stubs.

What are your priorities?

POSTING DATE │ 24 OCTOBER 2016

HUMANlongevity

You are approaching your 100th birthday. Life is good and you are healthy thanks to advances in medical science. But your retirement savings are anything but healthy. In fact, they're almost depleted. You quit work 40 years ago and are about to outlive your savings.

If the above scenario sounds frightening, then brace yourself as it may become increasingly common in future decades. Human longevity is constantly rising and a growing number of people are expected to have life spans beyond 100 years. Some, however, will run out of money before they run out of life.

Science is slowing the aging clock and keeping us alive longer and both these factors are adding years to our lives. Aging and age-related diseases are receiving greater attention and funding. Consequently, we are now living longer and healthier lives than at any point in human history.

All societies face the opportunities and challenges of how to help individuals reap the benefits of this additional time. Policymakers will increasingly be required to grapple with intergenerational demands from up to four generations co-existing, each with disparate needs.

A report prepared by the World Economic Forum, *Global Population Ageing: Peril or Promise?*, underscores that in both developed and developing countries, global aging will dramatically alter the way that societies and economies work. The report's preface states that:

> The issues (surrounding aging) include how individuals find fulfilment, at what age they retire, and their quality of life once they do retire; how governments devise social contracts to provide financial security; how the older and younger generations interact as they divide up the economic pie; how businesses staff their jobs to compensate in many countries for shrinking workforces; and how health systems respond to the altered needs of those living longer.

The report warns that if leaders fail to plan adequately for the changes ahead, they will be inundated by the effects of global aging. Such consequences include a dearth of workers, strained pension systems and overburdened health care systems. However, in line with the report's overarching optimism, it goes on to say that:

> the good news is that if we act now, in a creative and proactive manner, we will have the greatest chance of realizing the potential benefits of the aging trend – such as utilizing the immense social capital of older people – while avoiding its perils.

There is no doubt in my mind that science will continue to help us cheat death. All humans, of course, have an expiration date but medical advances are pushing back the boundaries of average life expectancy. The world now has 450,000 centenarians and that number is rising annually.

According to the Federal Government's 2015 *Intergenerational Report*, Australians will live longer and continue to have one of the longest life expectancies in the world. In 2054–55, life expectancy at birth is projected to be 95.1 years for men and 96.6 years for women. This compares with 91.5 and 93.6 years respectively today.

The grey tsunami sweeping the planet is pushing us into unchartered demographic waters. Today, there are more people over the age of 60 than children under five. According to a report by the United Nations Population Fund, just under two people celebrate their sixtieth birthday every second around the world – an annual total of almost 58 million sixtieth birthdays.

As the current cohort of baby boomers retire, I believe that one of our greatest challenges will be to discard our stereotypes of what it is to be old. Mature-age Australians are fitter, healthier and more active than any previous generation. Yet there remains a view that you can't teach an old dog new tricks.

The aging of our societies is one of the greatest success stories of the twentieth century. But adding wrinkles to the populace brings with it much more than just aesthetic change. Around the world, you will see an increase in the retirement age, a decrease in savings and a tightening in the eligibility criteria for welfare.

Aging is the reality for the future world and nations will need to respond accordingly.

POSTING DATE │ 13 JUNE 2017

TECHNOLOGICAL
ADVANCES
4

Technology is rapidly changing and expanding in every field. The gadget-filled 21st century is replete with iPhones, Kindles, laptops, tablets and electronic wallets. Technology – particularly the Internet – has transformed how we shop, pay for things and communicate. People are connected and empowered as never before with gadgets that are slimmer, faster and more energy efficient. In this final chapter we look at, inter alia, the rise in robot workers, the increasing use of algorithms, the application of block-chain technology and the development of quantum computing.

ROBOTworkers

In our staff kitchen here at Gateway, we have a coin-operated vending machine. It dispenses drinks and snacks. You could argue that it is taking away someone's job, but no one seems to care. Perhaps that's because it is viewed as a machine and not a robot. That's not to suggest that every robot is viewed as a threat.

A futuristic cruise ship which recently made Sydney its home port boasts a bionic bartender. Patrons customise their orders on a tablet screen and collect their cocktail at the bar in just thirty seconds. The twin robotic arms stir, shake and pour cocktails. This technology is a hit with passengers, even though the robot bartender is putting human bartenders out of work.

In Japan, an increasing number of firms are introducing robots as a solution to the country's rapidly shrinking workforce. They are appearing everywhere – from banks to factories – and are warmly embraced by colleagues and citizens. Japan is using its technological prowess to pioneer solutions for an aging population and now boasts the world's first hotel staffed by robots.

Beyond cruise ships and outside of Japan, there is considerable anxiety about robots replacing human workers. But is this fear rational? There is no doubt that some jobs will be automated, but many others will continue to need a human touch. However, if you use Google to search for information about artificial intelligence, it will return multiple sites predicting a robot takeover of the workforce.

Apparently, very few workers will escape the robot revolution unscathed. Millions of human jobs are allegedly destined for the scrap heap to be replaced by an army of robots that never strike or get sick. One US expert, Professor Moshe Vardi of Rice University, believes that the rise of robots could lead to unemployment rates greater than 50 per cent.

The robot revolution is not confined to manufacturing. Robots are leaving the factory floor and marching into our offices. Professional workers are also supposedly under threat. Professor Lynda Gratton of London Business School and futurologist David A. Smith boldly predict that robotics may make many lawyers, doctors and accountants redundant in 20 years.

Automation is also washing over into the armed services. Michael Horowitz, a University of Pennsylvania professor, is an expert on weaponised robots. He believes that over time the US military will "remove soldiers from non-combat deployments where they might face risk from adversaries on fluid battlefields, such as in transportation".

In a 2015 report, Bank of America predicted that robots and other forms of artificial intelligence will take over 45 per cent of all jobs in manufacturing by 2025. More recently, accountancy firm Deloitte predicted that a quarter of all jobs in the service sector are at high risk of automation within the next two decades.

Try as I might, I cannot embrace the doomsday predictions of mass redundancies due to humanoid robots. Respectfully, I think we have all watched too many sci-fi movies. I don't buy the hysterical robo-apocalypse scenario. Robots are not going to make us all technologically unemployed nor are they going to shatter the global economic order.

Regular readers of this blog know that I am not afraid to swim against the tide of popular opinion. When it comes to the unmitigated praise surrounding new technology, I am a true doubting Thomas. In previous posts, I have taken counter positions to the overhyped predictions regarding the take-up of Bitcoin, Google Glass and Apple Watch (to name but a few) and have been proven correct in each case.

Today, I am again sticking my neck out and going on the public record in saying that "expert" forecasts of robots putting over a billion people out of work are greatly exaggerated. As always, only time will tell if I am right. But I draw comfort from a 2016 report prepared by the Organisation for Economic Cooperation and Development (OECD).

You have to look hard to find this report as it has not captured the headlines. Perhaps this should not come as a surprise as its conclusions are not alarming. According to the OECD, only 9 per cent of jobs are at high risk of being replaced by machines by 2020. The report notes that "the risk of job loss because of automation is less substantial than sometimes claimed".

The OECD came to this conclusion due to the methodology it used. Whereas other reports look at broad occupations and whole classes of activities, the OECD analysed "the task content of individual *jobs* instead of the average task content of all jobs in each *occupation"*. In other words, it stripped jobs down into individual tasks.

In doing this, the OECD was able to identify which tasks are routine and repetitive and therefore ripe for automation and which tasks – like creativity, imagination and social interaction – cannot be replicated by machines. This process led the OECD to conclude that "automation and digitalization are unlikely to destroy large numbers of jobs".

Automation will displace some jobs but, according to the McKinsey Global Institute, not as many and not as fast as some fear. My sense is that the greatest impact of robots will be to transform jobs rather than replace human work. Certainly, the human workforce will not become obsolete. Indeed, automation will spur the growth of new jobs that don't currently exist.

My bet is that artificial intelligence/automation will create more than it destroys. Here's hoping!

POSTING DATE │ 8 MAY 2017

ROBOTtax

At first blush, it seems a good idea. The suggestion by Bill Gates to tax robots appears to have merit. Such a tax would help offset the falling revenues that will flow into public coffers as robots increasingly replace jobs held by humans. But on closer examination, the logic of a robot income tax turns out to be misguided.

The first problem you encounter is defining exactly what a robot is. Is an ATM a robotic worker? Are commercial washing machines robot employees? What about self-service petrol bowsers – are they job killers? If robotics is about automation, then virtually every machine in use today – from farm tractors to speed cameras – is a robot.

Of course, automation isn't new nor is our fear of it. In the early 19th century, English textile workers and weavers protested against the changes ushered in by the Industrial Revolution. These "Luddites" smashed mechanised knitting machines as they believed the new labour-saving devices would steal their jobs.

However, by the end of the 19th century, there were – according to James Bessen, author of Learning by Doing: The Real Connection between Innovation, Wages, and Wealth – four times as many factory weavers as there had been in 1830. Automation reduced labour costs for factory owners. This, in turn, enabled the price of garments to be lowered. This, in turn again, increased product demand leading to the need for more workers.

Retail behemoth Amazon provides a contemporary example of this phenomenon. A 2015 article by digital news site *Quartz* explained Amazon's hybrid workforce of people and robots this way:

> The company has over the last three years increased the number of robots working in its warehouses from 1,400 to 45,000. Over the same period, the rate at which it hires workers hasn't changed … robots help Amazon keep prices low, which means people buy more stuff, which means the company needs more people to man its warehouses even though it needs fewer human hours of labor per package.

Automation allows workers to deliver better, faster and cheaper services and that's good for growth and therefore good for the economy. If you tax automation, you are financially penalising companies for being technically innovative and that ends up hurting the economy. In the words of *The Economist* magazine:

> A robot is a capital investment, like a blast furnace or a computer. Economists typically advise against taxing such things, which allow an economy to produce more. Taxation that deters investment is thought to make people poorer without raising much money.

Most of us erroneously believe that our robotic co-workers will look like the humanoid C-3PO of Star Wars fame. Yet our factories and offices are already replete with robots – we just can't physically see many of them as they are in the form of automated systems. Robotic software is everywhere and is used to perform autonomous tasks.

Examples include expert systems (e.g. email spam filters), virtual assistants (e.g. Apple's Siri), and chatbots (e.g. Facebook's Messenger service). Other examples include the navigation system in our cars, the credit card fraud prevention processes run by banks and the surgical robots that assist doctors perform more accurate and less invasive procedures.

Should these non-human helpers be included in any proposed robot tax? Or should just some kinds of robotic automation be taxed? My belief is that no robot should be taxed. As James Bessen, writing in *FORTUNE* magazine, has asserted: "computer automation is actually increasing employment in most industries, so taxing robots would just slow job growth and limit economic opportunity for millions".

Bessen notes that barcode scanners, which were widely adopted in the 1980s, automated much of the work of cashiers, but the number of cashiers increased. Also, ATMs took over cash-handling tasks from bank tellers, but bank teller employment has continued to grow in the US. Similarly, speed cameras have not resulted in fewer police officers.

The central premise of Bill Gates' provocative suggestion is that robots should be taxed if they take people's jobs. But it's virtually impossible to categorically prove a direct correlation between the implementation of automation technology and job losses. Certainly, I have never encountered the situation where an organisation installs new technology on one day and then makes workers' roles redundant the next day.

While Mr Gates is a wise and astute businessman, the consensus is that he has got it wrong on this occasion. Each new wave of technology brings disruption and this creates winners as well as losers. But overall, history shows that automation brings more prosperity – and there's no reason to think that this time is any different.

POSTING DATE │ 21 AUGUST 2017

BASICincome

Both are tech billionaires, both are philanthropists and both have sounded dire warnings about job losses. Bill Gates and Mark Zuckerberg are concerned that technology and automation will eliminate millions of jobs around the world in the coming years.

In response, Bill Gates has recommended the introduction of a robot tax to fund other types of employment for those whose jobs are displaced by machines. Gates believes that the owner of a robot that takes your job should pay a robot tax to help retrain you.

Mark Zuckerberg, on the other hand, has recommended the introduction of a universal basic income to combat the rise in jobless workers. Zuckerberg believes that the spread of automation will require some kind of free pay cheque from governments – possibly funded by a tax on robots.

Last week, in my post *Robot tax*, I argued that requiring robots to pay income tax like any other employee is not a good idea. This week, I'd like to argue that an unconditional income paid by a government to all its citizens – regardless of whether they're in work – is equally not a good idea.

Let me firstly say that I understand the rising drumbeat of worry about robots taking human jobs. But as I pointed out in a recent post, *Robot workers*, I believe that the threat has been grossly exaggerated. According to the OECD, only 9 per cent of jobs are at high risk of being replaced by machines by 2020.

Even if the OECD is wrong and many more jobs are lost to automation, providing all citizens with a universal basic income is not the answer. Giving everyone free money – courtesy of the government – will not solve persistent unemployment or underemployment.

Most people want jobs, not handouts. The focus, therefore, should be on helping people adjust to change, just as we have since the Industrial Revolution. This is the very point made by US political commentator Rob Tracinski. In an opinion piece, he stated:

> helping people to adjust by putting them on a permanent welfare subsidy is the worst and cruelest response, precisely because it pays them *not* to adapt to the new economy.

Tracinski notes that the transition to the age of automation will not happen overnight. He says that people will have time to adapt as "the future doesn't come that fast". Workers should be encouraged to seek out the new jobs that will become available as the old ones fade away.

Tracinski acknowledges that the transition may be tough for some workers, adding that:

> it is harsh for those who are unable or unwilling to adapt and develop the new skills required for the new work. And that's precisely why the basic income is such a disastrous idea, because it is a massive disincentive for precisely that kind of adaptation.

Canadian academic Katharina Nieswandt takes a similar line to Tracinski. In her paper *Basic income after automation? That's not how capitalism works!,* Nieswandt observes that under capitalism, technological progress results in more products, not in more leisure. She states:

> Factories that improve their efficiency don't shut down and send workers home early – workers keep the same hours and crank out more goods …. The premise that automation will make human work superfluous flies in the face of all historical evidence. The dream that machines will someday do most work for us is almost as old as mankind.

In 1930, renowned British economist John Maynard Keynes wrote:

> We are being afflicted with a new disease of which some readers may not yet have heard the name, but of which they will hear a great deal in the years to come – namely, technolog-ical unemployment. This means unemployment due to our discovery of means of economizing the use of labor outrunning the pace at which we can find new uses for labor.

These sentiments confirm that our current anxiety over jobs being taken over by robots is not dissimilar to the fears of earlier generations. These fears led Keynes to make his now famous predictions that his grandchildren's generation (present day workers) would work only 15 hours per week.

A universal basic income has become a popular policy proposal, particularly among Silicon Valley luminaries. In addition to Mark Zuckerberg, Tesla CEO Elon Musk is also a vocal advocate of cash handouts as a social safety net in the form of a guaranteed monthly income just for being alive.

Call me old fashioned, but I still hold dear to the ideal of working hard to get ahead. Money for nothing is not the solution. Indeed, a stipend paid by the government to everyone smacks of socialism. This would move societies from having pockets of state dependency to all citizens (to varying degrees) becoming dependent on welfare.

I'll leave the final word on this well-intentioned but impractical idea to the Austrian Institute of Economics:

> A universal basic income is not the god-sent welfare policy that it initially seems to be. It does not create incentive to work. It won't help solve unemployment, and it will not alleviate poverty. The truth is that a UBI will exaggerate all of these factors in comparison to what would exist in a more unhampered market. There is even reason to think that it would be worse in the long-run than traditional, means-tested welfare systems.

POSTING DATE | 28 AUGUST 2017

CORPORATEgiants

Apple, Amazon, Facebook, Microsoft and Alphabet (the parent company of Google) are economic powerhouses. These tech behemoths have created an Internet oligopoly that has changed the face of modern capitalism. Collectively, their combined market capitalisation is worth three trillion dollars, making them the most valuable public companies on the planet.

Each is a digital superpower and undisputed ruler in their chosen market. Apple is the world's leading smartphone manufacturer. Amazon is the world's biggest online retailer. Facebook is the world's most popular social network. Microsoft is the world's largest software company. And Google is the world's dominant search engine.

Their phenomenal corporate might has led some commentators to dub them "the frightening five". Together, they control much of the critical digital infrastructure which underpins global commerce. Their products play a big role in our day-to-day lives and they are increasingly defining how we work, shop, bank, communicate and play.

The growing dominance of these colossal corporations is fuelling concerns about data privacy. The world's most valuable resource is now data, and Silicon Valley has cornered the market on amassing personal information. Apple, Amazon, Facebook, Microsoft and Alphabet each hold enormous pools of data about their users.

Quantifying the amount of data captured and stored by the big five tech firms is very difficult – but it is astronomical and this is what sets them apart. For example, 40,000 search queries are performed every second on Google and this equates to a staggering 1.2 trillion searches per year. Each search generates "data exhaust" – the trail of clicks that Internet users leave behind.

It is this data exhaust from Internet searches, smartphones and other connected devices that is enabling the big five to sweep up vast quantities of data about consumers' activities. This, it is said, puts them in the personal data extraction industry. A recent article in *The Guardian* explained how tech firms make money from monitoring everything we do.

> Companies harvest data by observing as much of our online activity as they can. This activity might take the form of a Facebook like, a Google search, or even how long your mouse hovers in a particular part of your screen. Alone, these traces may not be particularly meaningful. By pairing them with those of millions of others, however, companies can discover patterns that help determine what kind of person you are – and what kind of things you might buy. These patterns are highly profitable. Silicon Valley uses them to sell you products or to sell you to advertisers.

While surveillance capitalism is big business, critics argue that it destroys privacy and produces inequality. These concerns are picked up in Jonathan Taplin's book *Move Fast and Break Things: How Facebook, Google, and Amazon Cornered Culture and Undermined Democracy*.

Taplin notes that "not since Rockefeller and J.P. Morgan has there been such a concentration of wealth and power" in the hands of so few. He laments that "the enormous unprecedented fortunes created by the digital revolution have done much to increase inequality in America".

Unquestionably, the handful of men who have shaped the tech industry have been handsomely rewarded. Indeed, these titans now dominate the ranks of the world's wealthiest people. According to *Forbes* magazine's 2017 Rich List, the net worth of America's tech billionaires continues to grow:

- Microsoft visionary Bill Gates is the world's richest person ($86b).

- Amazon founder Jeff Bezos occupies the third rung ($72.8b).

- Facebook CEO Mark Zuckerberg sits in fifth position ($56b).

- Google pioneers Larry Page and Sergey Brin are in 12th and 13th place respectively ($40.7b and $39.8b).

Messrs Gates and Zuckerberg intend to give most of their respective fortunes away. Notwithstanding this philanthropy, many commentators believe that it is time to rein in America's five winner-take-all tech giants. There is growing concern that they are a threat – both economically and politically.

In any market, regulators like to see competition as this gives consumers choice. Having one dominant player lessens competition which typically leads to higher prices. But in the case of Google and Facebook, their services are free, thereby making concerns over pricing irrelevant. So the focus must be on whether there are other harmful economic effects.

As noted by *Bloomberg Technology*, companies like Amazon and Facebook are the middlemen for today's essential products and services, giving them leverage over both producers and consumers. The tech giants are also growing by snapping up potential rivals that might threaten market share. *Bloomberg* data shows that the big five have made 436 acquisitions worth $131 billion over the last decade.

The companies themselves say they are successful because of the quality of their offerings, so why punish success? To quote *Bloomberg*:

> Consumers appear to agree it's hard to beat Google's suite of free products or Amazon's convenience. Their dominance may not be about predatory practices so much as the nature of competition in the digital marketplace, where tech platforms benefit from network effects: As more people use them, the more useful – and dominant – the platforms become.

Politically, there is growing disquiet over the big five's influence over culture and information. For example, Facebook has become a global political force as the largest and most influential entity in the news business. *The New York Times Magazine* described Facebook as "the most powerful mobilizing force in politics". During the US election, propagandists used the service to turn fake stories into viral sensations.

The digital economy knows no national borders and this is a threat to the jurisdiction of governments around the world. Given this, we will likely see increasing friction between the big five companies that rule the tech industry and the governments that rule the lands those companies are invading. The nation-state is fighting not to lose its grip.

Love them or hate them, there's no escaping these tech superstars. They have become part of the fabric of our lives and will continue to cast a long shadow over the political, economic and social landscapes. For anyone in any doubt about their clout, I'll leave you with this sobering fact: If tech's big five were a nation defined by market value, it would rank as the world's fifth biggest economy – just ahead of the United Kingdom.

POSTING DATE | 18 SEPTEMBER 2017

ROBOThysteria

It's Arnold Schwarzenegger's fault. Ever since *The Terminator* was released in 1984, humans have been afraid of robots taking over the planet. Hollywood continues to feed the paranoia about artificial intelligence with a diet of movies portraying robots as evil machines.

Filmmakers know that people are predisposed to fear what they do not understand. Sci-fi movies about the future invariably tap into current anxieties and play to our primeval fears. One fear is that we will be replaced by machines and this resonates with workers. Many of us worry that flesh and blood employees will one day be supplanted by silicon and binary robots.

Since the Industrial Revolution, humanity has enjoyed a love-hate relationship with technology. Artificial intelligence has taken this to a new level with claims that human labour is under threat. With regular monotony, we are told that humanity is on a path to a jobless future.

I do not subscribe to the popular view that human workers will become obsolete. Indeed, I believe that everyone reading this blog can expect to keep on labouring until retirement. Headlines trumpeting "a world without work" are alarmist and underscore the long-standing divide between technologists and economists.

This is borne out in a September 2016 study by University of Melbourne labour-market economist Jeff Borland. Professor Borland accepts that the rise of robots makes for "a sexy story". But his study – *Are our jobs being taken by robots?* – reveals that there is absolutely no evidence "that computerisation is decreasing the aggregate hours of work done by labour in Australia".

Professor Borland acknowledges that "computerisation is changing the types of jobs being done by workers" but that its effect has been exaggerated. He states that "while computers may be having some impact on the Australian workplace, most claims about their impact are vastly over-stated".

Professor Borland is not alone in rejecting the view that a workless future is inevitable. Fellow labour-economist David Autor, from the Massachusetts Institute of Technology, sings from the same songbook. In his paper, *Why Are There Still So Many Jobs?*, Professor Autor contends that the skills required for many tasks – "that people understand tacitly and accomplish effortlessly" – cannot be readily codified.

Professor Autor observes "that journalists and even expert commentators tend to overstate the extent of machine substitution for human labor and ignore the strong complementarities between automation and labor that increase productivity, raise earnings, and augment demand for labor".

Another academic who believes that new technologies – such as artificial intelligence – are not the enemy of jobs is James Bessen, a professor of economics at Boston University. His research shows that emerging technologies often create new and higher-paying jobs that previously didn't exist – like social media managers.

Professor Bessen has found that automation can lead to the substitution of one occupation for another. For example, typesetting and compositor jobs in the US fell by about 100,000 during the 1980s. But from 1979 to 2007 the number of digital designers more than quadrupled to 800,000 due to the growth of desktop publishing.

So while typesetters may no longer be in demand, graphic designers are and their increased numbers more than compensate for job losses elsewhere. Professor Bessen has uncovered other examples where technology was supposed to annihilate jobs, but the opposite occurred. His findings are summarised in his article *'The Automation Paradox: When computers start doing the work of people, the need for people often increases'*.

One notable technologist who is on the right side of this emotive man-versus-machine debate is Steve Wozniak. The Apple co-founder is not worried that robots will become our overlords any time soon. In a CNBC article, *'Why robots won't be taking our jobs for hundreds of years'*, Wozniak is quoted as saying:

> This idea that computers could take over our jobs – because if they can think better, why have a CEO in a company? If a slow CEO costs you money, get rid of the CEO and have computers running the whole world – that's a theory. And I don't buy into it.

Wozniak is not losing sleep over humans becoming a "secondary species to machines" and neither am I. In my opinion, artificial intelligence should be seen as complementary to human expertise and not in competition with human endeavour.

It is important to make the distinction that technology eliminates jobs, not work. Technology made the job of buggy maker obsolete but created work for automobile manufacturers. While technology will continue to redefine work, it will not make humans unnecessary.

Those who assert that sapient robots will give rise to a personless workforce are overreacting. The coming automation of jobs won't play out as the doomsayers are predicting. The future of work is bright, not bleak, if we are prepared to change and constantly learn. It's up to all of us to upskill and reskill ourselves to keep up with the new and exciting jobs of tomorrow.

Be assured that robots are not job snatchers, but work creators – in fact, the biggest work creators in world history, according to a *Forbes* magazine article. So ignore the uninformed "robophobics" and make sure that you have the skills and capabilities necessary to thrive in a New Work Order.

Finally, in the words of *Star Trek* legend Mr Spock, *live long and prosper*. Or maybe I should have closed by paraphrasing the *Stars Wars* catchphrase – *may the (work) force be with you*. Unfortunately, I can't decide which one to use, so I'll end with *The Terminator's* iconic line – *I'll be back* (next week).

POSTING DATE │ 13 NOVEMBER 2017

BLOCKCHAINtechnology

Regular readers of this blog know that I am not a fan of Bitcoin and have long challenged its utility. Generating digital money using a computer has found some support among technophiles, but it has not been adopted into mainstream use. I firmly believe that fiat money will remain the currency of choice for the broader populace with Bitcoin as a bit player.

While the Bitcoin experiment has all but failed, it has left a positive legacy in the form of the underlying software architecture that drives Bitcoin – the blockchain. Just as it has been hard for people to get their minds around how Bitcoins are seemingly mined out of thin air, blockchain technology can also be a confusing concept and therefore needs some explaining.

At its most basic, a blockchain is a method of recording data. It's a digital ledger that verifies and records electronic events such as transactions, agreements and contracts. However, the ledger is not closed and centralised – as is normally the case – but open and decentralised.

Gateway operates closed and centralised ledgers – they are for our eyes only. They are not shared with anyone else due to privacy and confidentiality reasons. They are the definitive record of an individual's balances with Gateway and the one source of truth for member transactions.

In contrast, a blockchain ledger is not stored in one place. Rather, it is distributed across thousands of computers around the world. It is a replicated ledger of identical, publicly accessible transactions spread geographically across multiple sites, countries and institutions.

Okay, enough of the theory – let's look at a practical example. Let's say that today you want to transfer $100 from your account to a friend's account with a different financial institution. Your bank debits $100 from your account and your friend's bank credits her account with $100.

The two banks in question need to reconcile the two transactions and match them up. That involves a clearing house and settlement function in the middle. Routing transactions via a third-party settlement system is not lightning fast, which is why some payments take a couple of days to reach your account.

In the future, blockchain will facilitate these transactions in near real-time by eliminating virtually all back-end processing. Blockchain is a peer-to-peer system which requires no middleman. It will process payments in an entirely decentralised way, without the need for intermediaries such as banks.

Blockchain does not need to channel payments through clearing houses as it is a network of computers. These computers must approve a transaction that has taken place, before it is recorded in a "chain" of computer code. Every transaction is cryptographically chained to the previous transaction.

Once entered, the information is stored on a global network, so it can never be erased or tampered with. The distributed nature of a blockchain database means that hacking is almost impossible. Hackers would have to get access to every copy of the database simultaneously to be successful.

The disruptive technologies website *Nanalyze* puts it this way:

> All of these databases store a copy of the exact same dataset. These identical datasets are a ledger that contains every transaction that has ever taken place in chronological order. It's impossible to hack each and every database and change all these datasets at the exact same time so we can consider the dataset to be infallible, in other words, it always contains the truth.

The more technically minded reader might appreciate this explanation from the *Investopedia* website:

> A blockchain is … constantly growing as 'completed' blocks are added to it with a new set of recordings. A block is the 'current' part of a blockchain which records some or all of the recent transactions, and once completed goes into the blockchain as permanent database. Each time a block gets completed, a new block is generated. There is a countless number of such blocks in the blockchain. So are the blocks randomly placed in a blockchain? No, they are linked to each other (like a chain) in proper linear, chronological order with every block containing a hash of the previous block.

Blockchain technology is set to move into mainstream finance. It is seen as more secure, transparent, faster and less expensive than current financial systems. A group of major banks from around the world is working collaboratively to create a set of global standards for the use of distributed ledger technology in financial markets.

As a doubting Thomas, I have a track record of not buying into the unmitigated hype that typically surrounds new technology. However, I believe that the private replica of the Bitcoin blockchain technology being built by the banks has the potential to be a game-changer.

Blockchain may well transform how financial transactions are recorded, reconciled and reported. Get ready for a brave new world of banking.

POSTING DATE | 18 APRIL 2016

QUANTUMcomputing

Something exciting is happening in the world of computing. Scientists are developing computer technology based on the principles of quantum mechanics. This is a branch of science that deals with the physics of very small objects or, as some would say, an invisible world.

Classic (Newtonian) physics explains the things that we see and experience in our everyday world like the orbit of the planets or the motion of a car accelerating. Quantum physics, on the other hand, deals with atomic size particles and describes the behaviour of the universe on a much smaller scale, that of molecules, electrons and atoms.

Quantum physics looks at matter at its most fundamental level and produces results that are weird and unpredictable. A quantum computer taps directly into the strange and counter-intuitive world of quantum mechanics to speed computation. Experts claim that a quantum computer will be able to run calculations in a coffee break that would take a supercomputer of today millions of years.

In the words of the *WhatIs* technology website:

> Development of a quantum computer, if practical, would mark a leap forward in computing capability far greater than that from the abacus to a modern day supercomputer, with performance gains in the billion-fold realm and beyond. The quantum computer, following the laws of quantum physics, would gain enormous processing power through the ability to be in multiple states, and to perform tasks using all possible permutations simultaneously.

Now, if that explanation is too academic, try to get your mind around the example below from a prominent quantum computing scientist.

> Imagine you have only five minutes to find an "X" written on a page of a book in the Library of Congress (which has 50 million books). It would be impossible. But if you were in 50 million parallel realities, and in each reality you could look through the pages of a different book, in one of those realities you would find the "X."
>
> In this scenario, a regular computer is you running around like a crazy person trying to look through as many books as possible in five minutes. A quantum computer is you split into 50 million yous, casually flipping through one book in each reality.
>
> If this still sounds like magic or witchcraft, you're not alone. Physicist Richard Feynman once famously said: "If you think you understand quantum physics, you don't understand quantum physics".
>
> The bottom line is that regular computers have to solve one problem at a time in sequence, but quantum computers can solve multiple problems at the same time. That kind of speed has the potential to revolutionize entire industries.

One such industry is the medical sector. Developing a new drug is a complicated process. It requires chemists to test countless molecular combinations to find "the one" that has the specific properties that are effective against a disease. This process can take many years and cost millions of dollars.

Contrast this approach – which offers no guarantee of success as many molecular combinations fail during trials – with a quantum approach. A quantum computer would map out trillions of molecular combinations and quickly identify the ones that would most likely work, significantly cutting down the cost and the time of drug development.

The rules that govern the micro quantum world are radically different from those of the macro Newtonian world, with the latter providing our traditional understanding of binary logic in a computer. A conventional computer functions by storing data in a binary number format. This results in a series of 1s and 0s retained in electronic components such as transistors. Each component of computer memory is called a *bit.* A grouping of eight bits equals one *byte*.

Quantum computers do not work on *bits* and *bytes* but use *qubits*. A *qubit* is an electron in a magnetic field and can store a 0, a 1; both 0 and 1; or an infinite number of values in between – and be in multiple states (store multiple values) at the same time. This bizarre situation is called a "quantum superposition" and enables quantum computers to consider and manipulate all combinations of quantum bits simultaneously.

The Australian science communication website *Nova* describes the quirky rules that govern quantum computing this way:

Quantum laws are based on probabilities, so a computer on this scale no longer works in a 'deterministic' manner, which means it gives us a definite answer. Rather, it starts to behave in a 'probablistic' [sic] way – the answer the computer would give us is based on probabilities, each result could fluctuate and we would have to try several times to get a reliable answer.

Whether or not you understand how superfast quantum computers will work, they are going to change everything. I suspect that most mere mortals (me included!) will never truly comprehend superposition and the ability of a quantum system to be in multiple states – that is, "here" and "there", or "up" and "down" – simultaneously.

I'll leave the final word on quantum computing to British scientist Chris Woodford:

Quantum computing is hugely more complex than traditional computing and operates in the Alice in Wonderland world of quantum physics, where the "classical," sensible, everyday laws of physics no longer apply.

Hope that clears things up!

POSTING DATE | 20 JUNE 2016

DRONEtechnology

From delivering packages to tracking hurricanes, drones are increasingly part of our everyday lives. These unmanned aerial vehicles are not a passing fad as their potential uses continue to skyrocket. As drone technology becomes less expensive and more user-friendly, sales are predicted to soar.

In war-torn Syria, delivery drones drop food to starving villages. In Amsterdam, ambulance drones deploy defibrillators to patients within a 12-square kilometre zone inside of 60 seconds. In Sydney, surveillance drones spot sharks off beaches to protect swimmers and surfers from potential attack.

Farmers use drones to check fields for disease, spray pesticide and watch over livestock. Engineers use drones to inspect difficult to access infrastructure such as the underside of bridges and the tops of skyscrapers. Search and rescue teams use drones fitted with infrared technology to locate missing or injured persons by locking onto their heat signature.

Beyond the myriad civilian applications of drones, they are – of course – used by the military. Indeed, the first pilotless aircraft were built during World War I. Since that time, their growing high-tech sophistication has seen them come to prominence on modern battlefields. More and more countries are incorporating armed drones into their military arsenals.

Once relegated to intelligence, surveillance and reconnaissance missions, combat drones are a new front-line in the war against terrorists and other enemies of the state. Indeed, remote-controlled combat is changing the character of war. A new breed of "pilot" – who never leaves the ground – uses a joystick to guide missile-carrying drones to their intended target thousands of kilometres away.

It's said that a military drone has the characteristics of a sniper – silently killing before the target even knows it's there. A drone can hover over its target for hours, transmit video feed of the scene below and then strike suddenly. A former CIA chief believes that drones represent "the most precise and effective application of firepower in the history of armed conflict".

Politicians are attracted to drone warfare as military personnel are safely ensconced behind flickering computer screens in control centres. Politicians are acutely aware that the public does not like to see young men and women sent overseas to fight in "needless" wars. Invariably, some combat personnel return home in coffins while others suffer physical and emotional injuries.

Drones allow governments to take out the bad guys without the need to put troops on the ground and in harm's way. This, some argue, makes it much easier for political leaders to opt for quick-fix drone warfare in lieu of undertaking more difficult diplomatic solutions. Drones lower the threshold for using lethal force and this is seen as one of their real dangers.

Civilian drones have also come in for justifiable criticism. There are two broad areas of concern: privacy and safety. A drone fitted with a high-powered zoom lens can capture a person's every move and this represents an infringement of privacy. In the words of one US senator: "The thought of … drones buzzing overhead and constantly monitoring the activities of law-abiding citizens runs contrary to the notion of what it means to live in a free society".

In addition to aerial trespassing, another drawback of drones relates to public safety. In the hands of the wrong people, drones can be used to commit crimes and even carry out terrorist attacks. Drones have been used for a range of nefarious purposes – by gangs to carry drugs, by burglars to "case" homes and by paedophiles to spy on children in playgrounds. In 2015, a teenager in the US strapped a semi-automatic handgun to a drone causing much controversy.

As time goes by, criminal elements within society will undoubtedly find further evil ways to use drones. However, a less sinister threat to public safety comes from a drone crash-landing. Some amateur drone operators have lost control of their remote-controlled flying machines, with the most famous incident being the downing of a drone on the White House lawn. An Australian aviation software expert believes it's only a matter of time before we have "death by drone".

The biggest fear of most people is of a drone being hijacked. One way to take control of a drone is to interfere with the GPS system it uses to navigate. Hackers use a technique called "spoofing" whereby they send a signal which impersonates the signal a drone had been receiving, effectively relinquishing control of the drone to the hijacker. The good news is that military drones use encrypted frequencies of the GPS which, purportedly, cannot be hacked.

Like all technology, drones are not good or bad in and of themselves. It all comes down to how they are used and that is determined by the behaviour of the people who control them. For example, a drone's aerial photographic capability can be used to capture breathtaking images of the landscape. Conversely, it can be used to take intrusive photos of a neighbour sunbaking topless in her private and secluded backyard.

Drones have the distinct ability to go where humans can't and this is what makes them both exciting and scary. Only time will tell how the "Game of Drones" plays out for society. My sense is that they will prove to be more of a valuable invention than a destructive toy. One thing is clear: good or bad, they are here to stay. So get ready for a sky full of drones.

POSTING DATE │ 17 APRIL 2017

UNDERSTANDINGalgorithms

Algorithms are increasingly impacting our everyday lives. Many are designed to predict and even alter human behaviour. A range of organisations use algorithms including Google to rank the web pages we view, Amazon to recommend books for us to read, banks to assess our credit worthiness for a loan, and online dating sites to find our perfect match.

At its most basic, an algorithm is a set of instructions for how to achieve something. That something can be as simple as baking a cake or as complex as forecasting long-range weather patterns. The former merely requires a pen and paper to record a list of ingredients while the latter needs a computer capable of processing intricate mathematical calculations.

So both humans* and computers use algorithms. They are detailed, step-by-step roadmaps for completing a task (e.g. a recipe for making food) or solving a problem (e.g. evaluating the exposure of organisms to climate change). Each specific situation has a discrete and self-contained sequence of events which are defined by the relevant algorithm.

Withdrawing cash from an ATM is an algorithmic process. An ATM is a computerised telecommunications device that is programmed to operate in accordance with pre-determined rules – e.g. maximum withdrawal limit and PIN

---

* Circa 1600 BC, the Babylonians developed the earliest known mathematical algorithms for factorisation and finding square roots.

attempts. Within these parameters, the ATM has a certain number of predefined actions that it can perform – verify PIN, dispense cash, issue receipt, show balance and retain card.

In computing, programmers write algorithms that tell a computer precisely what it needs to do. These algorithms leave no room for subjectivity or judgment. They handle data and take resulting actions in a fixed manner according to rigid criteria. The most complicated algorithms are found in science, where they are used to design new drugs and model the climate.

Algorithms typically use the past as an indicator of the future and they do this by sifting through enormous masses of data. This is referred to as predictive modelling and it's a technique being used by law enforcement agencies to forecast crimes. Forecasting where and when a crime is likely to occur is gaining considerable currency around the world.

An early developer of predictive policing was the University of Memphis. A team of criminologists and data scientists compiled crime statistics from across the city of Memphis and overlaid these with other datasets – such as social housing maps and outside temperatures. They then instructed the algorithms to search for correlations in the data to identify future crime hotspots.

On 4 August 2005, Memphis Police – guided by the outputs of data-crunching algorithms – made so many arrests over a three-hour period that they ran out of vehicles to transport the detainees to jail. Three days later, 1,200 people had been arrested across the city – a new police department record. The data-driven operation was hailed a huge success.

Arguably, the world's most famous mathematical formula is Google's PageRank algorithm. While the exact way Google organises search results remains a closely-guarded secret, the broad strokes of how the algorithm works are known. Google's trademarked algorithm assigns each web page a relevancy score.

The task of sifting through all those pages to find helpful information is monumental. Yet Google's search engine generates results in a fraction of a second thanks to its algorithm. It instantaneously identifies web pages that contain the keywords used in a search request and then assigns a rank to each page. Higher ranked pages appear further up in Google's results page.

Algorithms are also being used to save lives. Living kidney donors and medically compatible transplant candidates have been successfully matched using computer algorithms. These kidney exchange programs have overcome the traditional problem of a willing donor (usually a loved one) not being compatible with the intended recipient of their organ.

In the past, these unmatched donor-recipient pairs had nowhere to turn. Now, they can join other incompatible pairs on a kidney database that creates a chain of donors and recipients. By pairing a selfless donor – who originally wanted to donate to a family member who was not a match – with a complete stranger, the matching algorithm results in a greater number of transplants.

The use of algorithms also extends to financial markets. High-frequency automated stock trading relies on algorithms to decide – based on criteria related to price, timing, volumes, etc. – what and when to buy or sell. The system enables firms to execute more than 100,000 trades in a second for a single customer – a speed that is impossible for humans to match.

When driving your car, algorithms figure out the best route for you to take. The science of route planning pulls together information such as length of road, time of day, volume of traffic, speed limits and road blocks to generate an estimated time of arrival. Sat-navs determine the shortest distance from where we are to where we would like to go.

It's clear that we are living in an algorithmic society. These mathematical formulas will progressively make more decisions for us and help solve more of our problems. From what we read, to whom we date and how we invest, you will not be able to escape algorithms. And if there's not an algorithm for something already, there soon will be!

POSTING DATE │ 24 APRIL 2017

REINVENTINGtransport

How we get from point A to point B is set to change. The primary driver (pun intended) of this change will be driverless vehicles. Google and several car manufacturers – including electric car maker Tesla – are in a race to bring self-drive cars to our highways and byways.

Autonomous vehicles will come without a steering wheel and pedals and will include self-drive trucks, self-drive buses and self-drive taxis. Uber expects its fleet to be driverless by 2030. By then, Uber believes its service will be so inexpensive and ubiquitous that car ownership may be rendered obsolete.

It is claimed that our privately-owned cars sit idle for over 90 per cent of the time. Given this, motorists are being attracted to ride sharing services such as GoGet. Research by consulting firm Deloitte shows that car ownership is increasingly making less sense to many people.

Younger people in particular are progressively not even bothering to obtain a driver's licence. It is no longer seen as a rite of passage, with teens viewing cars more as appliances than aspirations. Certainly, they don't want the hassle of owning, parking and insuring a car.

Down the track it may well be that few of us will hold a driver's licence. We may all become back seat drivers. Instead of putting our hands on the wheel, we will use our fingers to click a few buttons on a smartphone to summon a driverless car to our door in minutes.

This, some argue, should make our roads less clogged as we embrace the automotive sharing economy. Self-driving cars will be able to travel closer together and faster, thereby increasing average speeds. And unlike human drivers, autonomous vehicles will not break the law.

The economic and social consequences of driverless cars are significant. They will lead to an urban transformation that will change the way we live and interact. The transition to this brave new world of ultra-cheap, on-demand transportation won't be painless and will have repercussions in many areas.

Insurance companies can expect a significant decline in premiums as cars become safer. Deaths and injuries will plummet as driverless cars electronically "talk" to each other to avoid collisions. The need for crash and disability insurance will diminish.

Car makers will need to reinvent themselves or risk becoming extinct. Self-driving cars will reduce the need for consumers to have their own vehicles. Less direct ownership, more car sharing and competition from new tech firms like Tesla, Google, and Apple will disrupt incumbent auto manufacturers.

Credit providers like banks will face reduced demand for car financing. Ride sharing companies are transforming consumer attitudes to car ownership. As access to on-demand driverless vehicles grows, consumers will further question the validity of car ownership to the detriment of auto loans.

Transport workers will suffer big job losses. The world may wave goodbye to millions of jobs – from truck drivers to taxi drivers and limousine chauffeurs. There will also be a knock-on effect to businesses linked to road transport such as roadside cafés, motels and petrol stations.

Urban design will undergo a facelift as driverless cars usher in radical changes to the type of infrastructure required in cities and suburbs. Public car-parks and private garages could well become redundant. There may be less need for traffic lights and more need for electronic vehicle chargers in streets.

Public transport may suffer a decline in patronage as commuters favour driverless cars. Using public transport allows us to do other things like read – but so will a self-driving car with the added benefit of privacy. Those who don't currently drive – like the elderly and disabled – may also be attracted to self-drive transport.

Government revenues from fines for traffic violations will fall significantly. Driverless cars will not speed, run red lights or park illegally. Traffic tickets may ultimately become a thing of the past. Governments will feel the fiscal pinch and will need to find new revenue sources to fill state coffers.

To be clear, all the above are likely scenarios. No one can say with 100 per cent certainty how driverless technology will actually change our world. What is clear is that the change will be transformational and on par with the introduction of the steam engine and electricity.

The change from horse-drawn carriages to motor vehicles a century ago turned the world upside down. Autonomous vehicles are set to do the same. Yet again, we will adapt but there will be winners and losers. Hang on for an interesting ride as the road to the future becomes driverless.

POSTING DATE | 7 NOVEMBER 2016

CYBERspeak

The word "cyber" is used as a prefix for many things that are scary. Menacing terms like cyber-warfare, cyber-terrorism, cyber-attack and cyber-intrusion are familiar to all of us. These neologisms trigger evocative images of death, destruction and chaos.

"Cyber" is now firmly entrenched in our language and mindset. The origin of the cyber prefix can be traced back to the 1940s when mathematician Norbert Wiener used it to coin the word *cybernetics* to describe the futuristic idea of self-governing computing systems. It has since spawned a multitude of cyber terms.

Today, it is a catchphrase to describe anything to do with the Internet and online activities. The cyber tag is everywhere and its popularity is growing. Our lexicon is now replete with cyber buzzwords covering everything from online shopping (cyber-Monday) to online behaviour (cyber-culture).

There's even a TV series with a cyber name. The popular crime franchise *Crime Scene Investigation* (*CSI*) tapped into the cyber craze and launched *CSI: Cyber*. In this latest *CSI* spinoff, the evidence is mostly electronic rather than physical. The show features cyber-cops and a cyber-psychologist who investigate cyber-crime.

Some argue that we are experiencing cyber-overload. The ubiquitous prefix has become a cliché and its overuse is rendering the term meaningless. The label "cyber" has risen to the level of "information superhighway" and "web 2.0" making it a target for ridicule.

According to Wikipedia, there are over 450 words that begin with cyber. Our cyber vocabulary continues to grow as more and more things are given a cyber-focussed name. We need a cyber decoder to understand terms like cyber-hygiene, cyber-hug and cyber-kittens.

Cyber has grabbed the attention of the mass media. News broadcasts regularly report on lurking cyber dangers. Meanwhile, newspapers feature alarming headlines like "cyber-criminals steal millions" or "cyber-bullying an epidemic". The media play to our fear of online technology and this causes cyber-angst.

A writer for the science and technology website *Gizmodo Australia* believes that the word cyber has become a "linguistic drug" and that many in society are hooked on it. He writes:

> If someone snatches a bag on the street, he or she is a criminal. If they snatch a database full of credit card info, they're a cyber-criminal. If a guard chases the bag snatcher, he's part of security. If a smart guy chases the internet thief, he's a cyber security expert.
>
> But here's the rub: both of the thieves are criminals, and both of the pursuers are security experts. The internet should have nothing to do with how the events are communicated: it was just a tool used in the crime.

A growing chorus of commentators believe that the word cyber has become debased and that we need to hack away at cyber overkill. A good starting place would be the US government. A 2016 article by digital news site *Quartz* analysed every mention of the word cyber in Congress from the year 2000.

The article makes interesting reading. There were 80 distinct uses of cyber as a prefix. Among the more obscure words uttered by political leaders were cyber-squatting, cyber-patriot, cyber-introverts, cyber-actor, cyber-area and cyber-tip.

You would be forgiven for thinking that cyber can be slapped in front of almost anything. Certainly, virtually everything related to the Internet can be prefaced with the word cyber. Cyber makes something sound more official or threatening.

Cyber enables you to create "cyber-this" and "cyber-that" simply by adding a suffix. It can mean everything and nothing. The *New York* magazine was quick to spot this utility and offered the following opinion in the 23 December 1996 edition of its magazine:

> Cyber is such a perfect prefix. Because nobody has any idea what it means, it can be grafted onto any old word to make it seem new, cool – and therefore strange, spooky.

One reason why cyber is overused is the lack of an easy substitute. Possible synonyms include electronic, networked, computerised, hyperspace and online. But none of these work as a prefix of evil or a prefix to support a salad of suffixes.

The good news is that our cyber-world won't face cyber-Armageddon if we can't find a word to replace cyber. This may annoy pedants who cringe at awkward sounding cyber words. However, my sense is that cyber is here to stay as it's now part of the vernacular.

To quote a September 2016 article in the *New York* magazine:

> "Cyber" is an inescapable part of our technological vocabulary. It's impossible to get the cyber-toothpaste back in the cyber-tube.

On that basis, I should inform you that this blog was written with the help of a cyber-machine. So perhaps I should call this online column a cyber-blog. Just a cyber-thought!

POSTING DATE │ 12 MARCH 2018

HUMANbanking

The customer experience landscape is changing. Our digital world has made it possible for an increasing number of organisations to offer 24/7 service. The old 9–5 x 5 operating model is rapidly becoming a thing of the past. But customers are not bits and bytes and still require a human touch. This certainly holds true in banking.

A mobile banking app can provide only a finite amount of help or reassurance. Customers still need to discuss issues with a banking professional who can offer advice. Humans add value and can display empathy which is why human-to-human interaction will never be completely replaced by machines. Only another human can satisfy our deep interpersonal needs.

As I have repeatedly opined in this blog, banking is all about relationships, which is why machines should only be used to automate repetitive or low-value tasks. Attempts to automate high-value tasks invariably meet with failure. An example is the decade-long project in Australia to fully automate the end-to-end mortgage application and settlement process.

The mistaken belief by many in the Australian banking industry was that borrowers wanted a seamless mortgage process without any human intervention. In reality, almost 55 per cent of Australians turn to a mortgage broker to find the mortgage that's right for them. This is borne out in research which confirms that borrowers value hand-holding when taking out a home loan.

Automating decision-making processes in banking can lead to poor outcomes. Indeed, the absence of human judgment can cause embarrassment to both a financial institution and its customers. Two such instances were noted in a 2014 article in *American Banker* titled 'Go Digital, But Don't Forget Banking's Human Factor'. It reported:

> When President Obama has his credit card rejected at a restaurant because of a fraud protection algorithm in his bank's computer system and when Ben Bernanke can't refinance his home, it's a sign that the banks have lost their human sensitivity. These experiences are not outliers; they are the norm.

Machines might be smart, but I believe that humans are smarter. Sure, artificial intelligence is outstanding at analytics (logical intelligence). But emotional intelligence is just as important for decision-making. We humans rely on nuanced readings of complex situations while machines have no such subtlety. When it comes to artificial intelligence, faster isn't necessarily wiser.

To this end, someone who does not believe that the bank of the future will be completely automated is Jean Dermine, professor of Banking and Finance at INSEAD. He notes that user adoption is an important psychological aspect to digital technologies:

> Just because you disrupt the field with a very advanced form of artificial intelligence doesn't mean people will trust it with their accounts, passwords or life savings. Yes, many people will

welcome the change, but I strongly believe that the human touch will always remain important to some people. In fact, human interactions may one day become a rare value-added feature, something that the high-net-worth customers are willing to pay extra for, while the less well-to-do have no choice but to have a fully automated account with no personal service.

Given the significant levels of wealth held by non-millennials around the world – particularly baby boomers – there is still a place for relationship banking. Some customer segments will continue to value the customer experience associated with familiar faces and working with people you know. Nonetheless, I accept that millennials will approach banking differently.

In this banking battle for the ages, no one size fits all. In the words of *The Financial Brand*, millennials and boomers are "the two largest generations in history (but) have vastly different financial needs and expectations". Hence, banks that act too rashly in replacing the human touch with digital channels risk alienating customers who crave a more human experience.

Digital may be alive and kicking, but personal interaction is not dead. The human touch still matters in a digital world.

POSTING DATE │ 30 OCTOBER 2017

TECHNOLOGY contrarian

It's not easy swimming against the tide of popular opinion. I've done that on occasions in this blog and have sometimes been criticised for my views. I've learned that challenging conventional wisdom makes you an easy target. But I refuse to be silenced by self-appointed experts who often turn out to be incorrect.

In this blog, I comment on contemporary political, economic, social and technological issues. And yes, I sometimes take a position that runs counter to predominant paradigms. But I rationally argue my case and explain how I reached my conclusion.

I never set out to be a contrarian when I started this blog in 2008. My simple aim was to educate and inform. But over time, I came to realise how often "experts" are mistaken. More disturbingly, their predictions are invariably taken as gospel – and not to be questioned by doubting Thomases like me!

However, I cannot "get on the bus" of prevailing sentiment if I believe that it's going in the wrong direction. To do so would compromise my integrity. Nonetheless, it's no fun being the odd man out. So when I offer an opinion that separates me from the pack, it's not done lightly.

Indeed, I always feel some trepidation when I go out on a limb, especially when it comes to technology. Disruptive innovation has few critics which is why I try to bring a measured dose of scepticism. As *Time* magazine has noted: "The graveyard of technology is riddled with failed products".

Over recent years there have been several novel innovations which have been proclaimed as game-changers by the acolytes of the tech industry. Many of these innovations have failed spectacularly to live up to the unwarranted exaggeration and fanfare that surrounded their introduction.

In this blog, I have commented on a number of these innovations – gadgets, gizmos and devices – that were hailed at the time as "the next big thing". However, I had a different take and saw them – quite rightly as it turns out – as the next big epic failure.

That Google Glass flopped, Apple Watch fizzled and Bitcoin flunked was not a surprise to me. Each was a solution in search of a problem which is why they failed to attract a critical mass of users. While every breakthrough is presented as a triumph, getting consumers to embrace new technology isn't easy.

Makers of wearable technology have learned that lesson. Predictions that wearables would rapidly go from high-tech novelty to everyday necessity have not materialised. As I opined in a September 2015 post: "I cannot see wearable technology becoming the new dress code for the masses any time soon".

My attitude to wearables has not changed – they still have a long way to go to become mainstream (if ever!). But for that to occur, there will need to be a merging of technology with fashion. Meantime, analysts continue to pump out reports trumpeting the prospects of the wearable technology sector.

Like wearables, my sense is that the forecast scale of adoption of open banking is also being exaggerated. I think that proponents are getting a little ahead of themselves in describing open banking as a financial revolution. It hasn't even been launched in Australia yet, so care needs to be exercised about counting chickens before they hatch.

Undoubtedly, some consumers will be attracted to open banking, but will it fundamentally change the financial landscape as some are claiming? The Federal Government – which intends to follow the UK and force banks to open their customer data to competitors – believes open banking will open the floodgates to new entrants to boost competition.

Australia's big four banks are understandably concerned about security and data privacy issues related to open banking. Moreover, recent research reveals that only seven per cent of Australians would be comfortable sharing their financial data with an Internet start-up. It would take just one major data breach under the new open banking regime to undermine trust and confidence in data sharing.

Techno-enthusiasts invariably hype technology well beyond what is reasonably justifiable. They expect things to go one way, but they often go another. High technology is filled with promise and peril and this creates a yawning gap between fact and fiction. The grim reality is that most new technology does not take the world by storm.

To be clear, I am neither Luddite nor high-tech heretic. On the contrary, I welcome innovation that solves human problems and makes our lives easier. But we must avoid uncritically embracing every new product idea just because it's technically possible. Overselling ideas benefits no one – remember the promise of the paperless office?

It's important that perspectives are challenged otherwise groupthink sets in and we all become conformists. Independent and critical thinking enables me to see black where others see white. As Mark Twain said: "Whenever you find yourself on the side of the majority, it is time to pause and reflect".

I do a lot of reflecting.

POSTING DATE │ 6 NOVEMBER 2017

SOCIALmedia

It seems that the world is hooked on social media. Billions of people use social networking sites like Facebook, Instagram, LinkedIn, Snapchat, Twitter and Pinterest to seek out information and interact with others. This has revolutionised the way we communicate and connect in a globalised world.

Every click, every view and every sign-up on the Internet is recorded and this has produced some mind-boggling statistics. Every day, 500,000 new users are added to Facebook, 80 million photos are uploaded on Instagram and 500 million messages are sent via Twitter. However, like all technology, social media is a double-edged sword.

Advocates of social media wax lyrical about its ability to bring people together. Networking sites help people find old friends and make new ones. Users can connect with family and friends by posting pictures and status updates. They can also access support groups, "meet" people with common interests and raise awareness for causes.

Opponents of social media argue that it makes us less sociable due to an absence of face-to-face communication. Also, it puts our lives on public display, opens the door to stalking and cyber-bullying and perpetuates false and unreliable information. Further, it turns some people into crushing bores as they publicly detail every insignificant aspect of their lives.

Researchers at Harvard University learned through a series of experiments that the act of disclosing information about oneself activates the same part of the brain that is associated with the sensation of pleasure. This, apparently, is the same pleasure that we get from eating food, obtaining money or even having sex.

This discovery goes some way to explaining why social media is highly addictive and can be as habit-forming as illicit drugs. Many people find it compelling to share everything about themselves and can't resist constantly going online throughout the day to check and interact on social sites.

According to the *2016 Social Media Report* by Sensis, just under 70 per cent of Australians are on social media. The report, *How Australian people and businesses are using social media*, reveals that Australians own an average of three Internet-connected devices. These devices are used by 57 per cent of Aussies to access social media every day or most days.

The break-up of device ownership among Australians is as follows:

- 76 per cent own a smartphone;
- 70 per cent own a laptop computer;
- 54 per cent own a desktop computer;
- 53 per cent own a tablet PC; and
- 29 per cent own Internet-enabled TVs.

Where Australians check their social media is also revealed in the Sensis report:

- 96 per cent at home;
- 35 per cent at work;
- 25 per cent on public transport; and
- 8 per cent at the gym.

93 per cent of Australians who use Facebook spend 8.5 hours a week on the site – the equivalent to a whole working day. Personally, I find it hard to believe that this amount of time online does not impact the quality of personal relationships. Having said that, 17 per cent of respondents to the Sensis survey said that they use social media to connect with new people – with 10 per cent of those connections for dating.

In February 2013, I published a blog post titled *Lonely planet*. In that post, I acknowledged that the seven billion humans on this Earth have never been more connected. Moreover, I stated that technology had collapsed the physical boundaries between people and that we are conducting more and more of our relationships online. I went on to say that:

> Technology is bringing us together but, para-doxically, it's literally keeping us apart. As we become more connected, we become more disconnected. Meeting face-to-face is being replaced by communicating keyboard-to-keyboard. It's quicker and less hassle to send a quick text message than to eyeball someone.

> The line between real life and screen life has become blurred. An increasing number of people spend their days walking around with their noses buried in their BlackBerrys and iPhones. Others shut out the world with iPods. We seldom speak with our next-door neighbours but "chat" incessantly with cyber friends we rarely see.

Given the continuing rise of social media over the past four years, I believe that our planet is lonelier today than it was in February 2013. According to a survey by the Australian Psychological Society, Aussies who spend more time on social media report higher levels of loneliness and negative emotions. In contrast, Australians with strong relationships and community involvement are happier individuals.

We humans are herd animals and a lack of attachment is not normal. Yet our contact with each other is becoming more and more superficial. We have broader but shallower friendships. Real flesh and bone friends who stick with you through thick and thin are hard to find while transient, online virtual friends seem to pop out of the cyber-world.

In our technologically driven world, genuine human connection remains central to the wellbeing of Australians.

POSTING DATE ⎪ 17 JULY 2017

ORBITING satellites

This year marks the 60th anniversary of the launch of Sputnik 1 – the Soviet probe that became the first man-made object to reach space. In the years since Sputnik 1 first beeped its way around our planet, more than 6,000 satellites have been launched. Of these, it's estimated that 3,600 are still in orbit, but only about 1,100 are operational.

Today, satellites are an integral component of our high-tech civilisation. Indeed, they make modern life possible and connect the Earth into one global village. Satellites – or to be more precise, the services they make possible – are used almost every day by everyone. They may be out of sight and out of mind, but your life would not be the same without satellites.

Communication satellites connect us with family and friends and facilitate phone communications for passengers on airplanes and ships. They are the main conduit of voice communication for remote areas, whether on land, sea or in the air. Communication satellites bounce radio, television, Internet data and other kinds of information from one side of Earth to the other.

Navigation satellites keep us from getting lost. We no longer need to ask for directions or consult a map thanks to the Global Positioning System (GPS). This is comprised of a group of 24 satellites which transmit signals to our GPS-enabled smartphones and to the sat-nav devices in our cars. Simply type in your destination and your navigation aid will plot a route.

Environmental satellites observe and monitor the global environment. They provide early warnings of potentially harmful weather patterns like tropical cyclones and enable scientists to follow the effects of phenomena like volcanic eruptions. Environmental information helps us better understand our planet and the climatic changes which are taking place.

Military satellites gather intelligence on enemy installations and formations on the ground. Spy satellites document weapons development, track military deployments, detect missile launches and show bomb-strike damage. In addition to surveillance and reconnaissance, spy satellites play an active role in territorial conflicts when used for target acquisition.

Satellites perform a wide array of functions. Without satellites, there would be a dramatic reduction in our ability to communicate, share information and conduct transactions. In a 2014 article, a UK insurance company outlined a nightmare scenario – a massive solar storm temporarily disabling all satellites – with the following consequences:

> At first, disruption seems minimal: TV stations are forced to stop broadcasting. But then the situation starts to get more serious. Planes around the world are grounded as airline pilots lose touch with air traffic controllers; the world's money markets stop trading; global communications systems fail; and power cuts begin. By the end of the day, governments, fearing public disorder, order the army onto the streets and impose curfews.

While the likelihood of simultaneously losing transmission with all satellites orbiting the Earth is (hopefully) remote, it does – quite rightly – occupy the minds of space infrastructure experts. A 2013 BBC article chronicled how a day without satellites might pan out.

At 8 a.m., TV and radio stations find that they are limited to local content. Foreign correspondents cannot be reached and networks are unable to broadcast international events. More concerning, the loss of global satellite communications has put the world in danger. A US-based pilot squadron loses contact with armed drones that they have deployed over the Middle East. Meanwhile soldiers, ships and aircraft around the world have been cut off from their commanders and are vulnerable to attack. Without satellites, world leaders are struggling to talk to each other to diffuse mounting global tensions.

At 11 a.m., presidents and prime ministers gather their crisis teams while a new threat to global stability begins to emerge – the loss of the Global Positioning System (GPS). Despite its name, GPS is not about maps – it's about time. GPS satellites are highly accurate atomic clocks in space, transmitting a time signal back to Earth. Our infrastructure is held together by time – from time stamps on complex financial transactions to the protocols that hold the Internet together. When the packets of data passing between computers get out of sync, the system starts to break down. Without accurate time, every network controlled by computers is at risk. The cloud begins to fail, web searches become slower, traffic lights and railway signals default to red and mobile phone services fail.

By 4 p.m., aviation authorities ground commercial aircraft. Without weather satellite data, a storm system develops rapidly over the ocean and is missed by aircraft that fly straight into it. The severe turbulence leaves several passengers injured with the remainder badly traumatised. Around the world, other travellers are stranded thousands of miles from home.

As the clock strikes 10 p.m., the full impact of the "day without satellites" has become apparent. Communications, transport, power and computer systems have been severely disrupted. Global business has ground to a halt and governments are struggling to cope. Politicians are warned that food supply chains will soon break down. With fears of a breakdown in public order, governments introduce emergency measures.

The BBC article concludes with the sobering observation that the world would be in greater turmoil the longer the disruption to satellite transmissions lasts. One can only hope that this doomsday scenario never becomes a reality. We really do live in the space age and those chunks of metal orbiting overhead make our connected world possible. Long may they spin around our planet.

POSTING DATE ∣ 10 APRIL 2017

AFTERWORD

[FROM VOLUME 1]

Please allow me to begin this ending with an adage from legendary English writer Samuel Johnson: "A writer only begins a book. A reader finishes it." Thank you for getting to the end of this book. Dr Johnson also said that "the two engaging powers of an author are to make new things familiar and familiar things new". I hope that I have done just that.

The tale of how *Bite Size Advice* came to be can be traced back to late 2007. At that stage, Gateway Credit Union was redesigning its website and my then Head of Marketing, Loyce Cox-Paton, informed me that the new site would have provision for a CEO blog. My immediate response was to ask, "What's a blog?"

I was told that a blog is a form of self-publishing which enables you to share your thoughts and ideas with people online via a publicly accessible journal. After I digested what that meant I said, "Thanks, but no thanks." But Loyce persisted and I reluctantly agreed to start blogging. My first blog post was published on 25 March 2008 and is reproduced here:

> I must confess to feeling a tad nervous. I'd never heard of a blog 12 months ago. Yet here I am today sharing my thoughts publicly. I've always considered myself a frustrated writer, so I'm happy to accede to the wishes of my executive colleagues and give blogging a go.
>
> I've had a crash course in blogging and think I understand the rules of the game. It's been drilled into me that CEO blogs are not for corporate spin but for honest opinions. My aim is to write my blogs in a conversational style to facilitate open, two-way communication.
>
> The danger that all leaders face is receiving only filtered feedback. With the best of intentions, sometimes the bad news does not get to the CEO. Of course, the real boss in any organisation is the customer and I'm keen to hear from our members and potential members.
>
> So please use this new communication medium to tell me what you think. I have broad shoulders, so you can be frank. If we've made a mistake or fallen short in our service delivery, I'll unreservedly apologise. However, I'll draw the line at feedback which is unnecessarily rude or profane.

Well, I have never received offensive feedback on my blog and my readership continues to grow. A new reader to my blog about three years ago was Katherine Owen. Katherine and I met a short time earlier at an industry event and following that she subscribed to my blog.

I caught up with Katherine in the latter part of 2014 and she serendipitously informed me that she had started her own publishing company. Harbouring a life-long desire to publish, I seized the opportunity and asked Katherine if she would consider publishing the blog in book format and to my delight she agreed.

The first step in the blog to book process was obtaining the approval of my board of directors. My blog is not a personal blog but a corporate blog, written by me in my capacity as CEO of Gateway Credit Union[*]. I thank the board for approving my request and acknowledge each of my directors viz, Catherine Hallinan, John Flynn, Steve Carritt, Mal Graham, Graham Raward and Rene van der Loos.

Little did I know that the next step on the road to publishing would be so difficult. Katherine told me that the ideal word count for my book was 50,000 to 60,000 words. That meant I had to cull about 200 of the 300 blog posts I had written. The culling process straddled a three-week period and occurred in three stages. At the end of the third cull, I was within Katherine's word count limit.

My final challenge was to sort the remaining 100 posts into common themes so that they could form chapters.

---

* Now Gateway Bank.

My first two attempts at sorting the blogs into subject categories proved futile. Then, after a week of quiet reflection and contemplation (to keep a lid on my frustration!), the answer hit me – sort the blog posts using a PEST framework.

For the uninitiated, a PEST analysis is a simple and widely used tool that helps a business to evaluate the impact that Political, Economic, Social and Technological issues may have on its operations. To my delight, I found that the blog posts could be categorised into one of the four PEST areas and these became the thematic book chapters.

I continue to blog and publish a new post every Monday morning (Sydney time). Those readers wishing to follow my blog and receive the latest blog content can do so using the RSS subscription button at www.gatewaybank. com.au/CEOBlog.

RESOURCE LIST

This resource list acknowledges my debt to the many and varied sources of data and ideas I drew upon in researching and writing the 65 blog posts contained in this book. The list is arranged under the medium of publication and each citation includes sufficient information – including a URL where appropriate – to allow that source to be located and retrieved.

PUBLISHED BOOKS

Aigner, Geoff and Skelton, Liz. 2013. *The Australian Leadership Paradox: What It Takes To Lead In The Lucky Country*. Sydney: Allen & Unwin.

Bessen, James. 2015. *Learning by Doing: The Real Connection between Innovation, Wages and Wealth*. New Haven: Yale University Press.

Büthe, Tim and Mattli, Walter. 2011. *The New Global Rulers: The Privatization of Regulation in the World Economy*. New Jersey: Princeton University Press.

Gardner, Dan. 2010. *Future Babble: Why Expert Predictions Fail - and Why We Believe Them Anyway*. Melbourne: Scribe Publications Pty Ltd.

Hakim, Catherine. 2011. *Honey Money: The Power of Erotic Capital*. London: Penguin Books Ltd.

Hamermesh, Daniel S. 2011. *Beauty Pays: Why Attractive People Are More Successful*. New Jersey: Princeton University Press.

Hamilton, Clive and Denniss, Richard. 2005. *Affluenza: When Too Much Is Never Enough*. Sydney: Allen & Unwin.

Norberg, Johan. 2003. *In Defense of Global Capitalism*. Washington: Cato Institute.

Rhode, Deborah L. 2011. *The Beauty Bias: The Injustice of Appearance In Life and Law*. New York: Oxford University Press.

Stone, Gerald. 2007. *Who Killed Channel 9?: The death of Kerry Packer's mighty TV dream machine*. Sydney: Pan Macmillan.

Tanner, Lindsay. 2011. *Sideshow: Dumbing down democracy*. Melbourne: Scribe Publications Pty Ltd.

Taplin, Jonathan. 2017. *Move Fast and Break Things: How Facebook, Google, and Amazon Cornered Culture and Undermined Democracy*. New York: Little, Brown and Company.

The Economist. 2016. *Pocket World in Figures*. 25th anniversary edn. London: Economists Books.

NEWSPAPER ARTICLES

Bennett, Drake. 2008. 'Paradigm lost - Economists missed the brewing crisis. Now many are asking: How can we do better?'. *The Boston Globe* (online). 21 December.

Available: http://archive.boston.com/bostonglobe/ideas/articles/2008/12/21/paradigm_lost/

Bessen, James. 2016. 'The Automation Paradox: When computers start doing the work of people, the need for people often increases'. *The Atlantic* (online). 19 January. Available: https://www.theatlantic.com/business/archive/2016/01/automation-paradox/424437/

Bremner, Brian. 2015. 'Japan's Shinzo Abe hopes 'robot revolution' can replace ageing workforce'. *The Sydney Morning Herald* (online). 29 May. Available: https://www.smh.com.au/business/japans-shinzo-abe-hopes-robot-revolution-can-replace-ageing-workforce-20150529-ghc7ng.html

Browne, Andrew. 2016. 'U.S. Workers to Lose in China Trade War'. *The Wall Street Journal* (online). 15 November. Available: https://www.wsj.com/articles/u-s-workers-to-lose-in-china-trade-war-1479188319

Bump, Philip. 2016. 'Donald Trump took 5 different positions on abortion in 3 days'. *The Washington Post* (online). 3 April. Available: https://www.washingtonpost.com/news/the-fix/wp/2016/04/03/donald-trumps-ever-shifting-positions-on-abortion/?utm_term=.6f5fd2f619f9

Chang, Kenneth. 2017. '7 Earth-Size Planets Orbit Dwarf Star, NASA and European Astronomers Say'. *The New York Times* (online). 22 February. Available: https://www.nytimes.com/2017/02/22/science/trappist-1-exoplanets-nasa.html?_r=0

Confessore, Nicholas and Yourish, Karen. 2016. '$2 Billion Worth of Free Media for Donald Trump'. *The New York Times* (online). 15 March. Available: https://www.nytimes.com/2016/03/16/upshot/measuring-donald-trumps-mammoth-advantage-in-free-media.html

Crawford, Krysten. 2017. 'Stanford study examines fake news and the 2016 presidential election'. *The Stanford Daily* (online). 18 January. Available: https://news.stanford.edu/2017/01/18/stanford-study-examines-fake-news-2016-presidential-election/

Devine, Miranda. 2015. 'Welcome to Australia: the world's most over-regulated nanny state'. *The Daily Telegraph* (online). 12 August. Available: https://www.dailytele-graph.com.au/rendezview/welcome-to-australia-the-worlds-most-overregulated-nanny-state/news-story/49aa0a414ae87b9ef54e85b40af36b47

Graham, David A. 2017. 'Alternative Facts: The Needless Lies of the Trump Administration'. *The Atlantic* (online). 22 January. Available: https://www.theatlantic.com/politics/archive/2017/01/the-pointless-needless-lies-of-the-trump-administration/514061/

Graham, Ruth. 2013. 'Who will fight the beauty bias?'. *The Boston Globe* (online). 23 August. Available: https://www.bostonglobe.com/ideas/2013/08/23/who-will-fight-beauty-bias/Kq3pbfOy4VRJtlKrmyWBNO/story.html

Gebelhoff, Robert. 2016. 'Donald Trump's foreign policy inexperience is a true liability'. *The Washington Post* (online). 11 November. Available: https://www.washing-tonpost.com/news/in-theory/wp/2016/11/11/donald-trumps-foreign-policy-inexperience-is-a-true-liabili-ty/?utm_term=.c2c400d3d105

Han, Misa. 2017. 'Cash in circulation at 50-year high'. *Australian Financial Review* (online). 13 December. Available: http://www.afr.com/news/economy/cash-in-circulation-at-50year-high-20171213-h03pj4

Heath, Allister. 2013. 'The world has never had it so good - thanks partly to capitalism'. *The Telegraph* (online). 29 October. Available: https://www.telegraph.co.uk/finance/economics/10412499/The-world-has-never-had-it-so-good-thanks-partly-to-capitalism.html

Hickman, Leo. 2013. 'How algorithms rule the world'. *The Guardian* (online). 2 July. Available: https://www.theguardian.com/science/2013/jul/01/how-algorithms-rule-world-nsa

Holley, Peter., Ohlheiser, Abby and Wang, Amy B. 2017. 'The Doomsday Clock just advanced, thanks to Trump: It's now just 2½ minutes to midnight'. *The Washington Post* (online). 26 January. Available: https://www.washington-post.com/news/speaking-of-science/wp/2017/01/26/the-doomsday-clock-just-moved-again-its-now-two-and-a-half-minutes-to-midnight/?utm_term=.1de4f9b665a4

'IMF singles out Australia as global debt levels hit $US152 trillion'. *The Sydney Morning Herald* (online). 6 October 2016. Available: https://www.smh.com.au/business/the-economy/imf-singles-out-australia-as-global-debt-levels-hit-us152-trillion-20161006-grvwd3.html

Ingram, Tess. 2017. 'Australian radio telescopes have the capability to find ET'. *Australian Financial Review* (online). 24 February. Available: http://www.afr.com/news/australian-radio-telescopes-have-the-capability-to-find-et-20170224-gukgec

Kitfield, James. 2016. 'The Knowns and Unknowns of Donald Trump's Foreign Policy'. *The Atlantic* (online). 19 November. Available: https://www.theatlantic.com/international/archive/2016/11/trump-foreign-policy-flynn-sessions-obama-isis-iraq-muslim/508196/

Knapton, Sarah. 2016. 'Robots will take over most jobs within 30 years, experts warn'. *The Telegraph* (online). 13 February. Available: https://www.telegraph.co.uk/news/science/science-news/12155808/Robots-will-take-over-most-jobs-within-30-years-experts-warn.html

Krugman, Paul. 2003. 'Lumps of Labor'. *The New York Times* (online). 7 October. Available: http://www.nytimes.com/2003/10/07/opinion/lumps-of-labor.html

_____ 2015. 'The case for cuts was a lie. Why does Britain still believe it? The Austerity delusion'. *The Guardian* (online). 29 April. Available: https://www.theguardian.com/business/ng-interactive/2015/apr/29/the-austerity-delusion

Luce, Edward. 2017. 'The US government is at a dangerous impasse, but the Republicans will do nothing'. *Australian Financial Review* (online). 18 May. Available: http://www.afr.com/news/politics/world/the-us-government-is-at-a-dangerous-impasse-but-the-republicans-will-do-nothing-20170517-gw7eut

Manjoo, Farhad. 2016. 'Why the World Is Drawing Battle Lines Against American Tech Giants'. *The New York Times* (online). 1 June. Available: https://www.nytimes.com/2016/06/02/technology/why-the-world-is-drawing-battle-lines-against-american-tech-giants.html

Olen, Helaine. 2013. 'Why the federal budget can't be managed like a household budget'. *The Guardian* (online). 27 March. Available: https://www.theguardian.com/money/us-money-blog/2013/mar/26/federal-budget-household-finances-fed

Perlez, Jane and Huang, Yufan. 2017. 'Behind China's $1 Trillion Plan to Shake Up the Economic Order'. *The New York Times* (online). 13 May. Available: https://www.nytimes.com/2017/05/13/business/china-railway-one-belt-one-road-1-trillion-plan.html

'ROBOT TAKEOVER: Machines to replace doctors and lawyers in just 20 years'. *The Daily Express* (online). 20 May 2016. Available: https://www.express.co.uk/news/uk/672206/robots-machines-replace-doctors-lawyers-20-years

Roubini, Nouriel. 2014. 'Economic insecurity and the rise of nationalism'. *The Guardian* (online). 2 June. Available: https://www.theguardian.com/business/economics-blog/2014/jun/02/economic-insecurity-nationalism-on-the-rise-globalisation-nouriel-roubini

Runciman, David. 2016. 'How the education gap is tearing politics apart'. *The Guardian* (online). 5 October. Available: https://www.theguardian.com/politics/2016/oct/05/trump-brexit-education-gap-tearing-politics-apart

Shapiro, Jonathan. 2015. 'What is a AAA credit rating and why does Australia need one?'. *The Sydney Morning Herald* (online). 30 April. Available: https://www.smh.com.au/business/investments/what-is-a-aaa-credit-rating-and-why-does-australia-need-one-20150430-1mwkrh.html

Soos, Philip. 2016. 'How Australian households became the most indebted in the world'. *The Guardian* (online). 15 January. Available: https://www.theguardian.com/business/2016/jan/15/how-australian-households-became-the-most-indebted-in-the-world

Spence, Peter. 2016. 'Robots will replace a quarter of business services workers by 2035, says Deloitte'. *The Telegraph* (online). 12 July. Available: https://www.telegraph.co.uk/business/2016/07/11/robots-will-re-place-a-quarter-of-business-services-workers-by-20/

Stiglitz, Joseph. 2013. 'Australia, you don't know how good you've got it'. *The Sydney Morning Herald* (online). 2 September. Available: https://www.smh.com.au/opinion/australia-you-dont-know-how-good-youve-got-it-20130901-2sytb.html

Tarnoff, Ben. 2017. 'Silicon Valley siphons our data like oil. But the deepest drilling has just begun'. *The Guardian* (online). 23 August. Available: https://www.theguardian.com/world/2017/aug/23/silicon-valley-big-data-extraction-amazon-whole-foods-facebook

'The BBC deals a blow to investigative journalism'. *The Telegraph* (online). 11 November 2012. Available: https://www.telegraph.co.uk/comment/telegraph-view/9668780/The-BBC-deals-a-blow-to-investigative-journalism.html

'The future of war is robots'. *Daily Mirror* (online). 25 February 2017. Available: http://www.dailymirror.lk/article/The-future-of-war-is-ROBOTS-124479.html

Ting, Inga. 2016. 'The government says it has a plan to fix the housing affordability crisis. This chart suggests it doesn't'. *The Sydney Morning Herald* (online). 5 September. Available: https://www.smh.com.au/business/the-economy/the-government-says-it-has-a-plan-to-fix-the-housing-affordability-crisis-this-chart-suggests-it-doesnt-20160902-gr7sbz.html

Valenzuela, Rebecca. 2013. 'Surplus of political rhetoric'. *The Sydney Morning Herald* (online). 9 August. Available: https://www.smh.com.au/education/surplus-of-political-rhetoric-20130809-2rluz.html

Vidal, John. 2013. 'Land grabs expand to Europe as big business blocks entry to farming'. *The Guardian* (online). 18 April. Available: https://www.theguardian.com/global-development/2013/apr/17/land-grabs-europe-big-business-farming

MAGAZINES & PERIODICALS

Bessen, James. 2017. 'Bill Gates Is Wrong That Robots and Automation Are Killing Jobs'. *Fortune* (online). 25 February. Available: http://fortune.com/2017/02/25/bill-gates-robot-tax-automation-jobs/

Blodget, Henry. 2007. 'Socially responsible investing is neither as profitable nor as responsible as advertised. But if you insist, here's how to do it right'. *The Atlantic Magazine* (online). October 2007 issue. Available: https://www.theatlantic.com/magazine/archive/2007/10/the-conscientious-investor/306192/

Bloomberg. 2017. 'Speculative Mania. Bitcoin Is More Likely to Appeal to Criminals Than Consumers, RBA Governor Says'. *Fortune* (online). 13 December. Available: http://fortune.com/2017/12/12/bitcoin-philip-lowe/

Bokhari, Kamran. 2017. 'China's One Belt, One Road Faces Pushback'. *Geopolitical Futures* (online). 21 November. Available: https://geopoliticalfutures.com/chinas-one-belt-one-road-faces-pushback/

'Business by numbers: Consumers and companies increasingly depend on a hidden mathematical world'. *The Economist* (online). 13 September 2007. Available: https://www.economist.com/node/9795140

Cahill, Kevin. 2011. 'Who owns the world?'. *New Statesman* (online). 17 March. Available: https://www.newstatesman.com/global-issues/2011/03/land-queen-world-australia

Chamorro-Premuzic, Tomas. 2015. 'Why Bad Guys Win at Work'. *Harvard Business Review* (online). 2 November. Available: https://hbr.org/2015/11/why-bad-guys-win-at-work

Conca, James. 2015. 'The Fukushima Disaster Wasn't Disastrous Because Of The Radiation'. *Forbes Magazine* (online). 16 March. Available: https://www.forbes.com/sites/jamesconca/2015/03/16/the-fukushima-disaster-wasnt-very-disastrous/#5a03fef86b2d

Davidson, Adam. 2015. 'Debunking the Myth of the Job-Stealing Immigrant'. *The New York Times Magazine* (online). 24 March. Available: https://www.nytimes.com/2015/03/29/magazine/debunking-the-myth-of-the-job-stealing-immigrant.html?_r=0

'Donald Trump's victory is a disaster for Republicans and for America'. *The Economist* (online). 7 May 2016. Available: https://www.economist.com/news/leaders/21698251-donald-trumps-victory-disaster-republicans-and-america-trumpu2019s-triumph

Eadicicco, Lisa., Peckham, Mat., Pullen, John and Fitzpatrick, Alex. 2017. 'The 20 Most Successful Technology Failures of All Time'. *Time* (online). 3 April. Available: http://time.com/4704250/most-successful-technology-tech-failures-gadgets-flops-bombs-fails/

Faure, Gaëlle, 2009. 'Why Doctors Are Giving Heroin to Heroin Addicts'. *Time* (online). 28 September. Available: http://content.time.com/time/health/article/0,8599,1926160,00.html

Horgan, John. 2016. 'Are Drone Strikes Really Making Us Safer?'. *Scientific American* (online). 15 March. Available: https://blogs.scientificamerican.com/cross-check/are-drone-strikes-really-making-us-safer/

'How One Pollster Correctly Predicted Both Trump's Victory and Brexit'. *Fortune* (online). 11 November 2016. Available: http://fortune.com/2016/11/11/pollster-brandseye-donald-trump-brexit-social-media/

Kapko, Matt. 2016. 'How social media is shaping the 2016 presidential election'. *CIO Digital Magazine* (online). 29 September. Available: https://www.cio.com/article/3125120/social-networking/how-social-media-is-shaping-the-2016-presidential-election.html

_____ 2016. 'Twitter's impact on 2016 presidential election is unmistakable'. *CIO Digital Magazine* (online). 3 November. Available: https://www.cio.com/article/3137513/social-networking/twitters-impact-on-2016-presidential-election-is-unmistakable.html

'King: ace or joker? The report card on Sir Mervyn King'. *The Economist* (online). 31 March 2012. Available: https://www.economist.com/node/21551440

Kruse, Michael and Weiland, Noah. 2016. 'Donald Trump's Greatest Self-Contradictions'. *Politico Magazine* (online). 5 May. Available: https://www.politico.com/magazine/story/2016/05/donald-trump-2016-contradictions-213869

Lincicome, Scott. 2016. 'Donald Trump's China trade plan would make American families pay a lot more for food, clothing, electronics, and everything else that now says 'Made in China'.' *The Federalist* (online). 20 January. Available: http://thefederalist.com/2016/01/20/almost-everything-donald-trump-says-about-trade-with-china-is-wrong/

Manjoo, Farhad. 2017. 'Can Facebook Fix Its Own Worst Bug?'. *The New York Times Magazine* (online). 25 April. Available: https://www.nytimes.com/2017/04/25/magazine/can-facebook-fix-its-own-worst-bug.html

Mann, Charles C. 2011. 'Smoke screen'. *Vanity Fair* (online). 20 December. Available: https://www.vanityfair.com/culture/2011/12/tsa-insanity-201112

'Out of ammo? Central bankers are running down their
     arsenal. But other options exist to stimulate the
     economy'. *The Economist* (online). 20 February 2016.
     Available: https://www.economist.com/news/leaders/
     21693204-central-bankers-are running-down-their-
     arsenal-other-options-exist-stimulate

Oxenham, Simon. 2016. 'What explains Brexit, Trump and
     the rise of the far right?'. *New Scientist* (online). 4 July.
     Available: https://www.newscientist.com/
     article/2095975-what-explains-brexit-trump-and-the-
     rise-of-the-far-right/

'Politicians and central bankers are not providing the world
     with the inflation it needs; some economies face
     damaging deflation instead'. *The Economist* (online). 23
     October 2014. Available: https://www.economist.com/
     news/briefing/21627625-
     politicians-and-central-bankers-are-not-providing-
     world-inflation-it-needs-some

Schlegel, Jeff. 2017. 'Inspire ETFs Take Their Cue From
     The Bible'. *ETF Magazine*. (online). 3 March. Available:
     https://www.etfa-mag.com/news/inspire-etfs-take-their-
     cue-from-the-bible-31669.html

Silverstein, Michael J. and Fiske, Neil. 2003. 'Luxury for the
     Masses'. *Harvard Business Review* (online). April 2003
     Issue. Available: https://hbr.org/2003/04/
     luxury-for-the-masses

Snowdon, Christopher. 2015. 'Australia's shark-punching
     outlaw spirit is losing its battle with the nanny state'.
     Spectator (online). 4 August. Available: https://health.
     spectator.co.uk/australias-shark-punching-outlaw-
     spirit-is-losing-its-battle-with-the-nanny-state/

'Stimulus v austerity: Sovereign doubts'. *The Economist*
     (online). 28 September 2013. Available: https://www.
     economist.com/news/schools-brief/21586802-fourth-
     our-series-articles-financial-crisis-looks-surge-public

Tamny, John. 2015. 'Why Robots Will Be The Biggest Job Creators In World History'. *Forbes Magazine* (online). 1 March. Available: https://www.forbes.com/sites/johntamny/2015/03/01/why-robots-will-be-the-biggest-job-creators-in-history/#65f1f9a2d46c

'The 45th president: What is Donald Trump likely to achieve in power?'. *The Economist* (online). 21 January 2017. Available: https://www.economist.com/news/leaders/21714990-what-donald-trump-likely-achieve-power-45th-president

'The economics of good looks: Pretty people still get the best deals in the market, from labour to love'. *The Economist* (online). 27 August 2011. Available: https://www.economist.com/node/21526782

'The greatest business decisions of all time'. *Fortune* (online). 1 October 2012. Available: http://fortune.com/2012/10/01/the-greatest-business-decisions-of-all-time/

'The promise of the blockchain - the trust machine: The technology behind bitcoin could transform how the economy works'. *The Economist* (online). 31 October 2015. Available: https://www.economist.com/news/leaders/21677198-technology-behind-bitcoin-could-transform-how-economy-works-trust-machine

'The role of technology in the presidential election: From fake news to big data, a post mortem is under way'. *The Economist* (online). 20 November 2016. Available: https://www.economist.com/news/united-states/21710614-fake-news-big-data-post-mortem-under-way-role-technology

Walsh, Bryan. 2013. 'The Triple Whopper Environmental Impact of Global Meat Production'. *Time* (online). 16 December. Available: http://science.time.com/2013/12/16/the-triple-whopper-environmental-impact-of-global-meat-production/

'What Trumponomics means for the border region'. *The Economist* (online). 13 October 2016. Available: https://www.economist.com/news/americas/ 21708666-its-not-just-wall-appals-what- trumponomics-means-border-region

'Why taxing robots is not a good idea'. *The Economist* (online). 25 February 2017. Available: https://www. economist.com/news/finance-and-economics/ 21717374-bill-gatess-proposal-revealing-about- challenge-automation-poses-why-taxing

MEDIA OUTLETS

Ball, Lewis. 2015. 'The hunt for ET will boost Australian astronomy'. *The Conversation* (online). 21 July. Available: https://theconversation.com/the-hunt-for- et-will-boost-australian-astronomy-44957

Barnes, Terry. 2016. 'We must restore the value of a mandate'. *The Drum* (online). 8 June. Available: http:// www.abc.net.au/news/2016-06-08/barnes-we-must- restore-the-value-of-a-mandate/7488748

Burgess, Melanie. 2017. 'Robots, automation, artificial intelligence not as scary for workers as they seem'. *News.com.au* (online). 24 February. Available: http:// www.news.com.au/finance/work/at-work/robots- automation-artificial-intelligence-not-as-scary-for- workers-as-they-seem/news-story/38b- cd6f730f0f8b36815d91d60bea8d1

Carney, Matthew. 2017. 'China wants 'new Silk Road' One Belt One Road project to help it dominate world trade'. *ABC News* (online). 14 May. Available: http://www.abc. net.au/news/2017-05-14/china-plans-new-silk-road-to- dominate-world-trade/8522682

Carvalho, Patrick. 2015. 'Why migrants may be our greatest economic asset'. *The Drum* (online). 21 April. Available: http://www.abc.net.au/news/2015-04-21/carvalho-why-migrants-may-be-our-greatest-economic-asset/6409042

Chung, Frank. 2015. 'Three things that make New Zealand better'. *News.com.au* (online). 16 April. Available: http://www.news.com.au/finance/economy/three-things-that-make-new-zealand-better/news-story/efb745fbae40c0dd14e444cdeb60b3fd

Clifford, Catherine. 2017. 'Apple co-founder Steve Wozniak: Why robots won't be taking our jobs for hundreds of years'. *CNBC* (online). 13 June. Available: https://www.cnbc.com/2017/06/12/apple-co-founder-steve-wozniak-why-robots-wont-be-taking-our-jobs.html

Collins, Keith. 2016. 'Government officials just really like the word "cyber"' *Quartz Media* (online). 5 March. Available: https://qz.com/631803/government-officials-just-really-like-the-word-cyber/

Curtice, John. 2016. 'EU referendum - how the polls got it wrong again'. *The Conversation* (online). 26 June. Available: http://theconversation.com/eu-referendum-how-the-polls-got-it-wrong-again-61639

Gahan, Peter. 2015. 'The $100 billion question: can Australia afford our retirement bill as the 'grey vote' booms?'. *The Conversation* (online). 18 May. Available: http://theconversation.com/the-100-billion-question-can-australia-afford-our-retirement-bill-as-the-grey-vote-booms-41492

Green, Jonathan. 2014. 'Our reckless media fans the flames of disquiet'. *The Drum* (online). 9 October. Available: http://www.abc.net.au/news/2014-10-09/green-our-reckless-media-fans-the-flames-of-disquiet/5799504

Heath, Michael. 2016. 'Worrying About Aussie AAA Is So 1980s as Economy Craves Stimulus'. *Bloomberg Markets* (online). 11 July. Available: https://www.bloomberg.com/news/articles/2016-07-10/worrying-about-aussie-aaa-is-so 1980s-as-economy-craves-stimulus

Henckel, Timo. 2017. 'What economics has to say about housing bubbles'. *The Conversation* (online). 3 April. Available: http://theconversation.com/what-economics-has-to-say-about-housing-bubbles-74925

Hollingham, Richard. 2013. 'What would happen if all satellites stopped working?'. *BBC Futures* (online). 10 June. Available: http://www.bbc.com/future/story/20130609-the-day-without-satellites

Jarvis, Darryl S.L. 2016. 'Donald Trump's presidency could be a disaster for the global economy'. *The Conversation* (online). 10 November. Available: http://theconversation.com/donald-trumps-presidency-could-be-a-disaster-for-the-global-economy-68551

Kessler, Sarah. 2017. 'The optimist's guide to the robot apocalypse'. *Quartz Media* (online). 9 March. Available: https://qz.com/904285/the-optimists-guide-to-the-robot-apocalypse/

Kozaki, Danuta and Stuart, Riley. 2017. 'Sydney housing: New survey paints dire picture for Harbour City's middle-income earners'. *ABC News* (online). 24 January. Available: http://www.abc.net.au/news/2017-01-24/sydney-housing-affordability-nightmare-laid-bare-in-survey/8206676

McKenzie, Sheena. 2015. 'Anna Kournikova: How a 'marketing monster' seduced the world'. *CNN International* (online). 28 November. Available: https://edition.cnn.com/2015/11/09/sport/anna-kournikova-tennis-sport-marketing-sponsorship/

McLaughlin, David. 2017. 'Are Facebook and Google the New Monopolies?: QuickTake Q&A'. *Bloomberg Technology* (online). 13 July. Available: https://www.bloomberg.com/news/articles/2017-07-13/antitrust-built-for-rockefeller-baffled-by-bezos-quicktake-q-a

McMah, Lauren. 2015. 'Biggest piece of property on Earth up for sale in Australia'. *News.com.au* (online). 29 June. Available: http://www.news.com.au/finance/real-estate/buying/biggest-piece-of-property-on-earth-up-for-sale-in-australia/news-story/1d718ac16b476794d54ee976455d30a4

Nicholls, Rob. 2016. 'The myth of economies of scale: bigger is not necessarily better for super funds' *The Conversation* (online). 31 May. Available: https://theconversation.com/the-myth-of-economies-of-scale-bigger-is-not-necessarily-better-for-super-funds-60177

Nieswandt, Katharina. 2016. 'Basic income after automation? That's not how capitalism works'. *The Conversation* (online). 7 October. Available: http://theconversation.com/basic-income-after-automation-thats-not-how-capitalism-works-65023

Phibbs, Peter and Gurran, Nicole. 2017. 'Why housing supply shouldn't be the only policy tool politicians cling to'. *The Conversation* (online). 14 February. Available: https://theconversation.com/why-housing-supply-shouldnt-be-the-only-policy-tool-politicians-cling-to-72586

Rasmussen, Mikkel B. 2014. 'Go Digital, But Don't Forget Banking's Human Factor'. *American Banker* (online). 17 November. Available: https://www.americanbanker.com/opinion/go-digital-but-dont-forget-bankings-human-factor

Ryan, Peter. 2015. 'Analysis: Sydney housing bubble threat presents challenges for Government, Reserve Bank'. *ABC News* (online). 1 June. Available: http://www.abc.net.au/news/2015-06-01/housing-bubble-threat-presents-challenges-for-government-rba/6513072

Scott, Malcolm and Sam, Cedric. 2017. 'Here's How Fast China's Economy Is Catching Up to the US'. *Bloomberg* (online). 6 November. Available: https://www.bloomberg.com/graphics/2016-us-vs-china-economy/

Smith, Warwick. 2014. 'Why the federal budget is not like a household budget'. *The Conversation* (online). 17 December. Available: http://theconversation.com/why-the-federal-budget-is-not-like-a-household-budget-35498

Timm, Jane C. 2016. 'The 141 Stances Donald Trump Took During His White House Bid'. *NBC News* (online). 28 November. Available: https://www.nbcnews.com/politics/2016-election/full-list-donald-trump-s-rapidly-changing-policy-positions-n547801

Verrender, Ian. 2015. 'Do we really deserve a AAA credit rating?'. *The Drum* (online). 18 May. Available: http://www.abc.net.au/news/2015-05-18/verrender-do-we-really-deserve-a-aaa-credit-rating/6476618

DIGITAL NEWS SITES

Beauchamp, Zack. 2017. 'How racism and immigration gave us Trump, Brexit, and a whole new kind of politics'. *Vox Media* (Online). 20 January. Available: https://www.vox.com/2016/9/19/12933072/far-right-white-riot-trump-brexit

Beauchamp, Zack., Dreazen, Yochi and Williams, Jennifer. 2016. 'The debate showed just how scary a Commander in Chief Donald Trump would be'. *Vox Media* (online). 27 September. Available: https://www. vox.com/2016/9/27/13068420/trump-debate-foreign-policy-hofstra

Blodget, Henry. 2013. 'The Economic Argument Is Over - Paul Krugman Has Won'. *Business Insider Australia* (online). 25 April. Available: https://www.businessin-sider.com.au/paul-krugman-is-right-2013-4

Brooks, Emily. 2016. 'Human Connection Trumps Social Media In Australia's Happiness Survey'. *Huffpost Australia*. (online). 3 November. Available: https:// www.huffingtonpost.com.au/2016/11/02/human-connection-trumps-social-media-in-australias-happiness-su_a_21597638/

Cohn, Jonathan. 2016. 'Donald Trump's Trade Plan Will Hurt The Very People He Promises To Help'. *Huffpost Australia* (online). 3 July. Available: https://www.huff-ingtonpost.com.au/entry/trump-trade-policy_us_577809eee4b09b4c43c0b2b0

Dickerson, Kelly. 2015. '7 awesome ways quantum computers will change the world'. *Business Insider Australia* (online). 22 April. Available: https://www. businessinsider.com.au/quantum-computers-will-change-the-world-2015-4?r=US&IR=T

Elumenu, Tony. 2013. 'Getting Paid, Not Aid: A Call to Revamp Aid in Africa'. *Huffpost* (online). 23 November. Available: https://www.huffingtonpost. com/tony-elumelu/getting-paid-not-aid-a-ca_b_3975595.html

'Impolite society: Who is to blame for Britain's bad manners?'. *Independent* (online). 26 May 2007. Available: http://www.independent.co.uk/news/uk/ this-britain/impolite-society-who-is-to-blame-for-brit- ains-bad-manners-5333186.html

Lee, Timothy B. 2016. 'The top 20 fake news stories outper- formed real news at the end of the 2016 campaign'. *Vox Media* (online). 16 November. Available: https://www.vox. com/new-money/2016/11/16/13659840/facebook-fake- news-chart

Littman, Michael. 2015. 'Rise of the Machines is Not a Likely Future (Op-Ed)'. *LiveScience* (online). 28 January. Available: https://www.livescience. com/49625-robots-will-not-conquer-humanity.html

Moore, Michael. 2016. 'Trump Is Self-Sabotaging His Campaign Because He Never Really Wanted The Job In The First Place'. *Huffpost* (online). 16 August. Available: https://www.huffingtonpost.com/mi- chael-moore/trump-self-sabotage_b_11545026.html

Pash, Chris. 2017. 'The Sydney housing market correction is coming'. *Business Insider Australia* (online). 10 April. Available: https://www.businessinsider.com.au/core- logic-moodys-the-sydney-housing- market-correction-is-coming-2017-4

Sachs, Jeffrey. 'The Path to Happiness: Lessons From the 2015 World Happiness Report'. *Huffpost* (online). Undated. Available: https://www. huffingtonpost.com/jeffrey-sachs/the-path-to- happiness-les_b_7127124.html

'Where polls failed, social media succeeded: Both Brexit and Trump'. *fin24 - BizNews* (online). 10 November 2016. Available: https://www.fin24.com/BizNews/ where-polls-failed-social-media-succeeded-both- brexit-and-trump-20161110

Worley, Will. 2017. 'New bill aims to ban Donald Trump from first use of nuclear weapons without Congressional Declaration of War'. *Independent* (online). 25 January. Available: http://www.independent.co.uk/news/world/americas/donald-trump-ban-use-nuclear-weapons-first-use-congressional-declaration-of-war-us-congressman-ted-a7545191.html

ASSORTED WEBSITES

Amy, Douglas J. Undated. 'The Deficit Scare: Myth vs. Reality'. *Government is Good* (online). Available: http://governmentisgood.com/articles.php?aid=30&p=1

Cahill, Kevin. 2007. 'Largest landowners'. *Who owns the world* (online). Available: http://www.whoownstheworld.com/about-the-book/largest-landowner/

Cole, Chris. 2014. 'What's wrong with drones?'. *Drone Wars UK* (online). 20 March. Available: https://dronewars.net/2014/03/20/whats-wrong-with-drones/

Gillin, Joshua. 2016. 'How Pizzagate went from fake news to a real problem for a D.C. business'. *PolitiFact* (online). 5 December. Available: http://www.politifact.com/truth-o-meter/article/2016/dec/05/how-pizzagate-went-fake-news-real-problem-dc-busin/

Haub, Carl. 2011. 'How Many People Have Ever Lived on Earth?'. *Population Reference Bureau* (online). October 2011. Available: http://www.prb.org/Publications/Articles/2002/HowManyPeopleHaveEverLivedonEarth.aspx

Hiscock, Michael. 2015. 'Dead Facebook users will soon outnumber the living'. *The Loop* (online). 26 June. Available: http://www.theloop.ca/dead-facebook-users-will-soon-outnumber-the-living/

Holan, Angie Drobnic. 2016. '2016 Lie of the Year: Fake news'. *PolitiFact* (online). 13 December. Available: http://www.politifact.com/truth-o-meter/article/2016/dec/13/2016-lie-year-fake-news/

Hopewell, Luke. 2014. 'Why You Sound Dumb When You Use The Word Cyber'. *Gizmodo* (online). 12 March. Available: https://www.gizmodo.com.au/2014/03/why-you-sound-dumb-when-you-use-the-word-cyber/

Howe, Marc. 2016. 'Why Supply Expansion Isn't a Panacea for Housing Affordability'. *Sourceability.net* (online). 15 September. Available: https://source-able.net/why-supply-expansion-isnt-a-panacea-for-housing-affordability/

Lawson, Greg R. 2016. 'For Trump, foreign policy should begin and end with China'. *The Hill Extra* (online). 3 December. Available: http://origin-nyi.thehill.com/blogs/pundits-blog/international/308646-for-trump-foreign-policy-should-begin-and-end-with-china?mobile_switch=standard

Luke, Jim, 2011. 'Private Debt vs Government Debt'. *ECONPROPH* (online blog). 14 July. Available: https://econproph.com/2011/07/14/private-debt-vs-government-debt/

'Open banking no fave in UK: Consumer research there indicates many don't trust fintechs'. *Banking Exchange* (online). 7 June 2017. Available: http://www.bankingexchange.com/news-feed/item/6931-open-banking-no-fave-in-u-k?Itemid=807

Parker, Thornton (Tip). 2016. 'Explaining Why Federal Deficits Are Needed'. *New Economic Perspectives* (online blog). 3 February. Available: http://neweconomicperspectives.org/2016/02/explaining-federal-deficits-needed.html

Phibbs, Peter and Gurran, Nicole. 2015. 'The five great myths about the Sydney housing market'. *Domain Group* (online). 31 August. Available: https://www.domain.com.au/news/the-five-great-myths-about-the-sydney-housing-market-20150831-gjap1c/

Ratner, Paul. (undated). 'How Many People Have Ever Lived on Planet Earth?'. *BigThink* (online). Available: http://bigthink.com/paul-ratner/how-many-people-have-ever-lived-on-planet-earth

Tracinski, Rob. 2016. 'The Basic Income Is the Worst Response to Automation'. *RealClear Future* (online). 15 August. Available: http://www.realclearfuture.com/articles/2016/08/15/basic_income_worst_response_to_automation_111934.html

van Onselen, Leith. 2017. '2017 Demographia Housing Affordability Survey'. *MacroBusiness* (online). 23 January. Available: https://www.macrobusiness.com.au/2017/01/2017-demographia-housing-affordability-survey/

INTERNATIONAL ORGANISATIONS

Dileep, George. 2016. 'No, the robots are not about to rise up and destroy us all'. *World Economic Forum* (online). 23 January. Available: https://www.weforum.org/agenda/2016/01/no-the-robots-are-not-about-to-rise-up-and-destroy-us-all/

'Global Population Ageing: Peril or Promise?'. *World Economic Forum* (online). 26 January 2012. Available: https://www.weforum.org/reports/global-population-ageing-peril-or-promise

Hofman, Bert. 2015. 'China's One Belt One Road Initiative: What we know thus far'. *The World Bank* (online). 12 April. Available: http://blogs.worldbank.org/eastasiapacific/china-one-belt-one-road-initiative-what-we-know-thus-far

Jaumotte, Florence., Koloskova, Ksenia and Saxena, Sweta Chaman. 2016. 'Impact of Migration on Income Levels in Advanced Economies'. *International Monetary Fund*. 24 October. Available: https://www.imf.org/en/Publications/Spillover-Notes/Issues/2016/12/31/Impact-of-Migration-on-Income-Levels-in-Advanced-Economies-44343

Jones, Brad. 2017. 'The Earth's population is going to reach 9.8 billion by 2050'. *World Economic Forum* (online). 29 August. Available: https://www.weforum.org/agenda/2017/08/the-earths-population-is-going-to-reach-9-8-billion-by-2050

Miksa, Brigitte. 2015. 'What are the economic consequences of rapidly ageing populations?'. *World Economic Forum* (online). 27 August. Available: https://www.weforum.org/agenda/2015/08/what-are-the-economic-consequences-of-rapidly-ageing-populations/

Organisation for Economic Co-operation and Development. 'Automation and Independent Work in a Digital Economy'. May 2016. Available: http://www.oecd.org/employment/Policy%20brief%20-%20Automation%20and%20Independent%20Work%20in%20a%20Digital%20Economy.pdf

Organisation for Economic Co-operation and Development. 'Is migration good for the economy?'. May 2014. Available: https://www.oecd.org/migration/OECD%20Migration%20Policy%20Debates%20Numero%202.pdf

THINK TANKS

Byman, Daniel L. 2017. 'Seven Trump foreign policy assumptions'. *The Brookings Institution* (online). 23 January. Available: https://www.brookings.edu/blog/order-from-chaos/2017/01/23/seven-trump-foreign-policy-assumptions/

Denniss, Richard. 2015. 'Who really makes legislation?'. *The Australia Institute* (online). 30 March. Available: http://www.tai.org.au/content/who-really-makes-legislation

Horwitz, Gabe and Chittooran, Jay. 2016. '50 Ways Trump Is Wrong on Trade'. *Third Way* (online). 7 April. Available: http://www.thirdway.org/memo/50-ways-trump-is-wrong-on-trade

Ikenberry, G. John. 2011. 'The Future of the Liberal World Order: Internationalism after America'. *Council on Foreign Relations* (Online). May/June issue of Foreign Affairs. Available: https://www.foreignaffairs.com/articles/2011-05-01/future-liberal-world-order

SCHOLARLY PUBLICATIONS

Arnold, Michael., Gibbs, Martin., Kohn, Tamara., Meese, James and Nansen, Bjorn. 2017. 'Communicating with the dead is closer than you might think, thanks to our online footprints'. *The University of Melbourne* (online). 16 July. Available: https://pursuit.unimelb.edu.au/articles/want-to-live-forever-here-s-how

Autor, David H. 2015. 'Why Are There Still So Many Jobs? The History and Future of Workplace Automation'. Massachusetts Institute of Technology. *Journal of Economic Perspectives,* Volume 29, Number 3 - Summer 2015 - Pages 3–30. Available: https://economics.mit.edu/files/11563

Borland, Jeff. 2016. 'Are our jobs being taken by robots?'. University of Melbourne, Department of Economics. *Labour market snapshot #31*. September 2016. Available: https://drive.google.com/file/d/0B_H1wGT-m98W3LUdwa0xYUV9xdU0/view

Cafaggi, Fabrizio. 2015. 'The Many Features of Transnational Private Rule-Making: Unexplored Relationships Between Custom, Jura Mercatorum and Global
Private Regulation'. University of Pennsylvania Legal
Scholarship Repository (online). *Journal of International Law*, Vol. 36, Issue 4, Art. 2, 24 September 2015.
Available: http://scholarship.law.upenn.edu/cgi/view-
content.cgi?article=1899&context=jil

Cummings, James. 2012. 'Working Paper: Effect of fund
size on the performance of Australian superannuation funds'. *Australian Prudential Regulation Authority*
(online). March 2012. Available: http://www.apra.gov.
au/AboutAPRA/Pages/Working-
Paper-Effect-of-fund-size-on-the-performance-
of-Australian-superannuation-funds.aspx

'International Law: 100 Ways It Shapes Our lives'
(booklet). *American Society of International Law*
(online). Available: https://www.asil.org/sites/default/
files/100%20Ways%20Booklet_2011.pdf

Krisch, Nico and Kingsbury, Benedict. 2006. 'Introduction:
Global Governance and Global Administrative Law in
the International Legal Order'. Oxford Academic (online).
European Journal of International Law, Volume 17, Issue
1, 1 February 2006, Pages 1–13. Available: Available:
https://academic.oup.com/ejil/article/17/1/1/411014

'Smart machines, smarter humans; the evolution of banking
in a digital world'. *INSEAD* (online). Interview with
Professor Jean Dermine. Available: https://www.insead.
edu/executive-education/interviews/banking/smart-
machines-smarter-humans-the-evolution-of-banking-
in-a-digital-world

Tulloch, Ian. 2008. 'Why Australia needs a less powerful
Senate'. *La Trobe University*. 2 July. Available: https://
www.latrobe.edu.au/news/articles/2008/opinion/why-
australia-needs-a-less-powerful-senate

SPEECHES

Obama, Barack. 2016. Address to the 71st Session of the United Nations General Assembly. September 20. Available: https://geneva.usmission.gov/2016/09/21/transcript-of-president-obamas-address-to-the-71st-session-of-the-un-general-assembly/

Richards, Heidi. 2016. 'A Prudential Approach To Mortgage Lending'. Paper presented to Macquarie University Financial Risk Day. 18 March. Available: http://www.apra.gov.au/Speeches/Documents/Mortgages%20Speech%20-%20Macquarie%20Risk%20Day%20March%202016.pdf

BUSINESS PUBLICATIONS

Hadley, James., Nielsen, Niels., Olsen, Thomas and Turner, Gary. 2015. 'The Return of Corporate Strategy in Banking'. *Insights - Bain & Co* (online). 2 September. Available: http://www.bain.com/publications/articles/the-return-of-corporate-strategy-in-banking.aspx

'Worldwide Cost of Living Report 2017'. *The Economist*. Intelligence Unit. Available: https://www.eiu.com/public/topical_report.aspx?campaignid=WCOL2017

'How Australian people and businesses are using social media'. *Sensis Social Media Report 2016*. Available: https://www.sensis.com.au/asset/PDFdirectory/Sensis_Social_Media_Report_2016.PDF

GOVERNMENT PUBLICATIONS

Migration Council of Australia. *'The Economic Impact of Migration'*. 2015. Available: http://migrationcouncil.org.au/wp-content/uploads/2016/06/2015_EIOM.pdf

ABOUT THE AUTHOR

Paul Thomas has worked in the financial services industry for over 40 years. His journey from bank teller to bank CEO began in 1976. He followed an old-fashioned career path that saw him rise through the ranks. Along the way, he gained broad experience in retail banking across a range of financial institutions.

Versed in all aspects of management, Paul is a high calibre executive with particular expertise in strategy development and execution. His deep knowledge of contemporary issues coupled with his passion for communication find expression in his weekly blog. He writes respectfully and insightfully – but without fear or favour – for the public at large.

Paul has developed a reputation as a thought leader and commentator on the contemporary political, economic, social and technological issues facing business and society. He offers informed insights and opinions in an authoritative voice that is authentic and engaging.

An accomplished public speaker and writer, Paul's credentials include an MBA and a Diploma in Financial Services. He is also a graduate of the Australian Institute of Company Directors.